simply POP

by tony jasper

Designer **Paul Chevannes**
Editor **Kate Ritchie**

All photographs by **Ian Dickson** unless otherwise credited
Front and back cover photographs: **Kate Simon:** Donny Osmond, Bay City Rollers, David Bowie, Rod Stewart, pop fans; **Ian Dickson**: Elton John, David Essex, Suzi Quatro; **Joseph Stevens:** Dave Hill.

Printed and bound in England by
Hazell Watson & Viney Limited, Aylesbury, Bucks

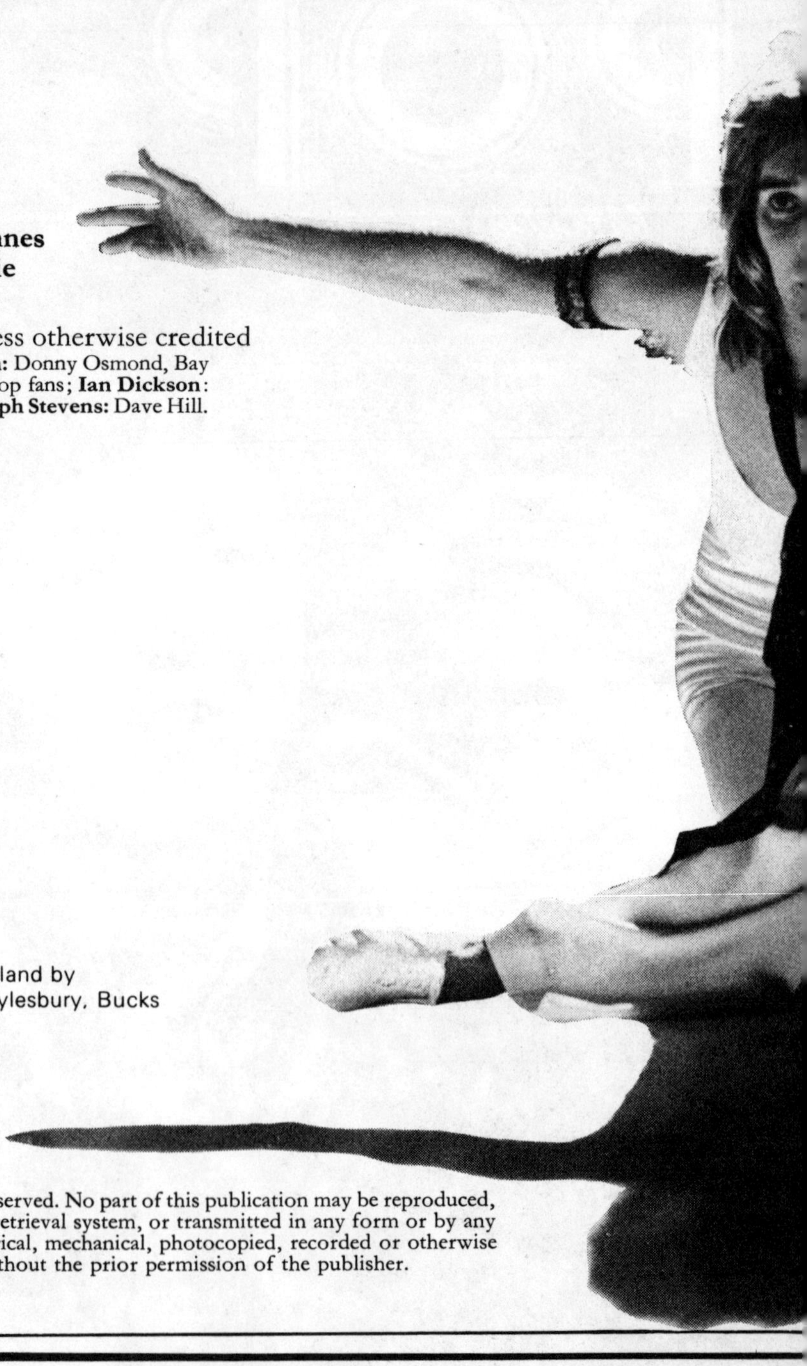

This book is dedicated to
some super teenagers called
Kathryn and Alan Wilson
and David Armstrong

ISBN 0362 00247 9

Published by Queen Anne Press Ltd
12 Vandy Street, London EC2A 2EN

contents

A TO Z

A

is for Ace; and The Average White Band who went from Scotland to America and found fame; and for Apple, The Beatles' record company which came to the end of the road in 1975.

B

is for BTO and the BCRs who have both come into the limelight in the last few years; the gentleman with a double B, Barry Blue; and Brutus and Ben Sherman which adorn so many pop fans.

C

is for Carshalton, where Mud come from; and for the American group, Chicago; plus 'commercial' radio stations which have enlivened our pop scene.

D

is for David of the white suits; and an old rock 'n' roll hero, Fats Domino; and those other two Davids, Bowie and Cassidy, who both seem to have disappeared for a while.

E

is for Essex of *Gonna Make You A Star*; and top American band, The Eagles; plus Eno, who was once with Roxy. And do you remember Engelbert?

F

is for glamorous Freddie of Queen; and the Dutch group Focus who recorded *Sylvia*; and the now-lamented group Family; and also for what might have been 1975's top pop film, *Flame*, which somehow didn't live up to expectations.

G

is for glasses and in particular those worn by Elton; and for Gary and The Glitter Band; and George of Beatle and religious fame.

H

is for Hello, the group which includes Bob Bradbury as a member; and for Steve Harley who had a couple of hits with Cockney Rebel in 1975; and for the Irish group Horslips, which has both Catholic and Protestant members.

I

is for Ian who was once with Mott and whose partner is now Mick Ronson, who originally found fame with David Bowie. I is also for Janis Ian who entered the charts when she was only 16 years old and people gossiped because in her song *Society's Child* she stated that a white girl could go out with a black boy.

J

is for The Jackson Five, if you can remember them! There's also Jim Gilstrap who auditioned with the 'flu but still won through and had a hit with *Swing Your Daddy*. J is also for a new group, Jet; plus all pop's Johnnies, not forgetting one in particular—the DJ Johnnie Walker, for all his excellent musical programmes on the radio.

K

is for The Kinks, a top group in the 1960s; and Kenny with the baggy trousers and coloured patches which were so cleverly designed by Colin Shepherd. Have you ever heard of The Kalin Twins? Check the record books!

L

is for Lyn, once of The New Seekers and who is now doing well as a solo artist; and Phil Lynott, the lead singer with Thin Lizzy; and of course London where all the leading record companies are to be found.

M

is for Manchester where 10CC and Sweet Sensation come from; and for Mutter who sometimes bangs dustbin lids for Stackridge.

OF POP

N is for Nutz, a group which is tipped for the top; and for Noddy of Slade, whose real name is Neville; *No Honestly*, the television theme music written by Lynsey de Paul; and for Gloria Gaynor's first big hit, *Never Can Say Goodbye*.

O is for a Band Called 'O'; and Nigel Olsson who was once the drummer with Elton's band; and for The Osmonds, who all appear to be getting married!

P is for Philadelphia where so many Soul records are recorded by artists such as The Three Degrees, Billy Paul, The Stylistics, Harold Melvin And The Blue Notes and The Detroit Spinners. There's also John Peel, who is also known as 'Peely' although his real name is John Ravenscroft; and it's also for Edinburgh's Pilot.

Q is for pop's only group which consists entirely of graduates, Queen; and for Suzi Q who doesn't always wear leather and who says that her variety of menus for cooking is very limited.

R is for *Rock On;* and *Remember Me This Way*, Gary's first film; and for The Rubettes, who once backed Barry Blue; and, of course, for the Rollers. Does anyone remember the old television pop show, *Ready Steady Go?*

S is for Sally of *Saturday Scene;* and Supertramp, a group which received recognition in 1975; and for Slade, the group in which every member owns a Rolls Royce; and for Susan Cadogan, the first librarian ever to have a record in the charts.

T is for The Three Degrees; and for Rob Davis' favourite Mud record *Tiger Feet*; and for television, on which so many pop shows, both good and bad, are screened.

U is for 'Uncle' as Neil Sedaka describes himself; and for *Under My Thumb*, a song resurrected from the past so successfully by Wayne Gibson.

V is for Frankie Valli, who recorded one of pop's biggest sleepers, *My Eyes Adored You*. Have you ever heard of Paul Vigrass?

W is for Wimbledon, the Common, and its resident pop group, The Wombles. W is also for Barry White, who is married to Glodean who is a member of his backing band, Love Unlimited; and for Wally, the band which was discovered by DJ Bob Harris.

X is for *Xanadu*, a hit record in 1968; but otherwise X is open to suggestions!

Y is for Kenny Young who discovered Noosha of Fox, and who also wrote tunes for the group; and for Yes, the group which once included Rick Wakeman as a member; and also for The Yardbirds, a group which many musicians remember and revere.

Z is for Frank Zappa, the leader of The Mothers of Invention; and for *Zig Zag*, the pop magazine; and for Zenda, a lovely lady.

So that's pop, from A to Z. Make up your own!

A STAR IS BORN

Do you know where your favourite pop people were born? Use this map to find out!

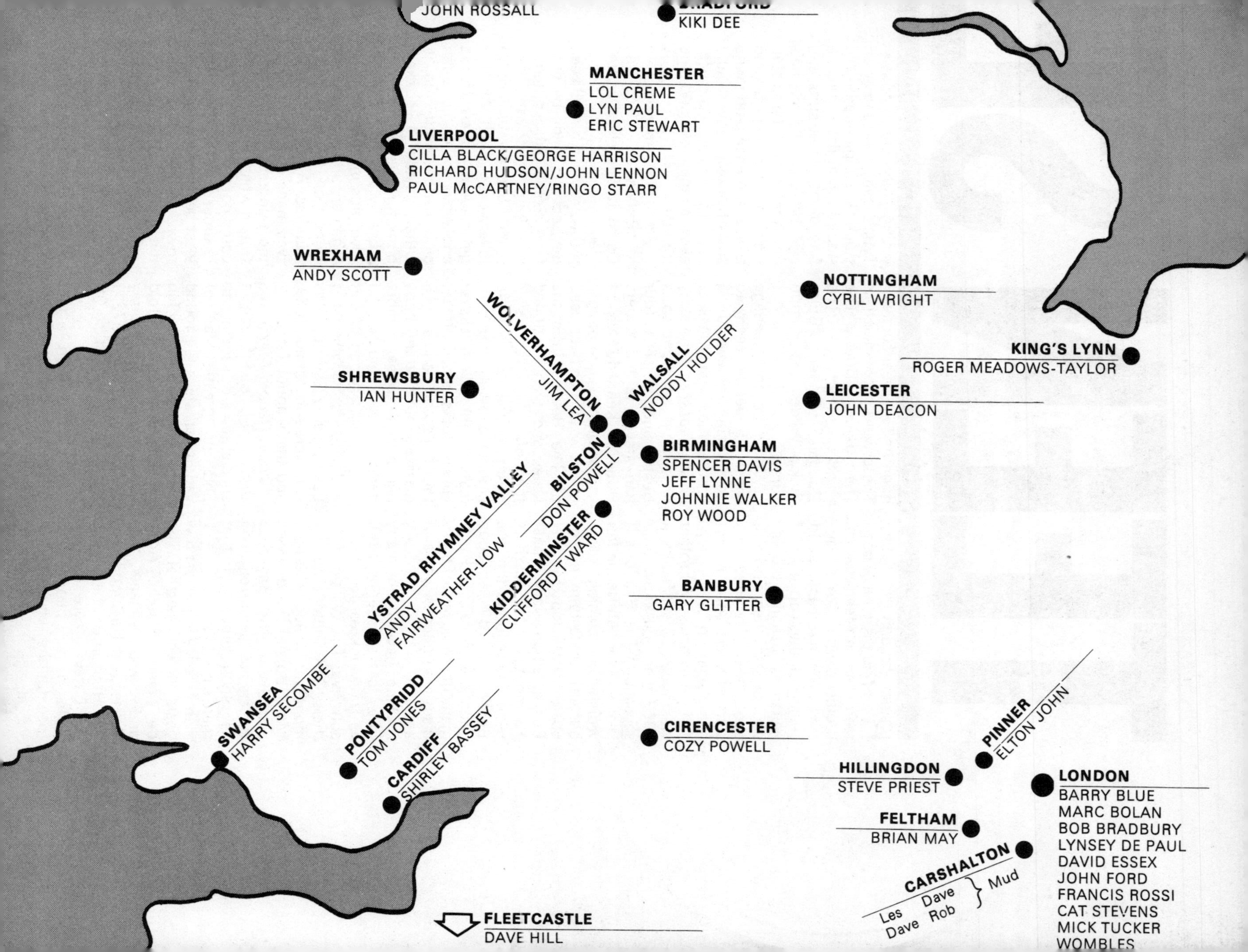

JOHN ROSSALL
KIKI DEE
MANCHESTER
LOL CREME
LYN PAUL
ERIC STEWART
LIVERPOOL
CILLA BLACK/GEORGE HARRISON
RICHARD HUDSON/JOHN LENNON
PAUL McCARTNEY/RINGO STARR
WREXHAM
ANDY SCOTT
NOTTINGHAM
CYRIL WRIGHT
KING'S LYNN
ROGER MEADOWS-TAYLOR
SHREWSBURY
IAN HUNTER
WOLVERHAMPTON
JIM LEA
WALSALL
NODDY HOLDER
LEICESTER
JOHN DEACON
BIRMINGHAM
SPENCER DAVIS
JEFF LYNNE
JOHNNIE WALKER
ROY WOOD
BILSTON
DON POWELL
YSTRAD RHYMNEY VALLEY
ANDY
FAIRWEATHER-LOW
KIDDERMINSTER
CLIFFORD T WARD
BANBURY
GARY GLITTER
SWANSEA
HARRY SECOMBE
PONTYPRIDD
TOM JONES
CARDIFF
SHIRLEY BASSEY
CIRENCESTER
COZY POWELL
PINNER
ELTON JOHN
HILLINGDON
STEVE PRIEST
LONDON
BARRY BLUE
MARC BOLAN
BOB BRADBURY
LYNSEY DE PAUL
DAVID ESSEX
JOHN FORD
FRANCIS ROSSI
CAT STEVENS
MICK TUCKER
WOMBLES
FELTHAM
BRIAN MAY
CARSHALTON
Les
Dave
Dave
Rob
Mud
FLEETCASTLE
DAVE HILL

TEEN SE

Right through the history of pop there have been teen stars and teen heroes. If older people look affronted by all the screaming and yelling, clothes copying and hairstyles just like the favourite star, then find out about *their* favourite film stars of years ago or your father's pin-up!

If your sister or brother was about 12 years old in 1962 then you know their sensation—The Beatles! It seems as though Beatle fan worship is coming back, because the album record charts have included several Beatles albums in the past 12 months. Shop owners have also reported that the Beatle record catalogue continues to sell, and that many of the buyers of these discs are under 16 years of age.

There have been many other teen sensations, such as The Monkees, The Jackson Five, The Walker Brothers, Gary Glitter, The Osmonds, David Cassidy, Marc Bolan, David Essex and Slade. The Bay City Rollers are the current teen sensation group, of that there's no doubt.

In America in the last few years we've heard of The de Franco Family, Andy and David Williams, The Sylvers, The Heywoods and The Hudson Brothers. Here in Britain there was a surfeit of teen people who tried for the limelight, but none had any real success. These were people such as The James Boys, The Handley Family, The Dougals, Darren Burn, Ricky Wilde and Simon Turner.

When it's real teenage sensation people seem to do anything and everything for their idols. Paul Krassner in *The Realist* told the story of a time he went to a Beatle auction. The four had stayed in the Riviera Hotel at Kennedy Airport and an organisation bought goods which had been used by The Beatles from the hotel, and then auctioned them off.

Among the goods were eight face towels; four bath mats; eight pillow cases; knives, forks, small plates; four cups and saucers; 16 glasses; four salt and pepper pots and many more items. How much did people pay? A pair of salt and pepper pots which had been used by George Harrison were sold for about $9, and that's about £4!

When *Record Mirror*, the British pop paper, ran a special award scheme to find the greatest fan of various artists, they found Julie Langram a worthy fan of The Osmonds. She told the paper, 'When Donny fell ill over here in 1972, I made him a 5ft 4in. by 3ft 6in. *Get Well* card!

In a competition to find Gary Glitter's greatest fan a young lady called Susan Tynan said that she even stuck Gary's picture on the side of a cornflakes packet. She owns glitter suits and said of Gary, 'To me he's much more than a pop star. He's a man. Flesh and blood. A human being who so obviously loves and cares for his fans. As much, even, as they love and care for him.'

When the Osmonds came to Britain in 1975 the Osmond fan club assembled a mass of special presents which had all been devised and made by their fans. Some girls knitted a mile-long scarf with their names and expressions of love woven into it. Another girl made a 12ft by 9ft rug and wove the Osmond fan club badge motif into it. Others made a cookery book for Mrs Osmond and a beauty volume for Marie. Two girls in York gathered together information for Donny on all the world's religions. A postcard chain was made consisting of all the hundreds of towns in Britain which The Osmonds could not visit on their tour, in order that they would at least see something of the towns which they had missed!

The people who work at The Osmonds record company remember well the crowds which gathered outside The Osmonds London hotel during one of

NSATION

their visits. Every entrance was watched by hundreds of fans. Some fans doubted the location itself and all hotels within the vicinity of the hotel into which The Osmonds were officially booked were subject to clusters of fans waiting outside day after day.

Some fans booked into the actual hotel as paying guests, but they failed to see The Osmonds for one reason—the hotel's lift was programmed not to stop at The Osmonds floor, and all stair entrances were guarded! Despite the cost of booking into a hotel, two fans did so when The Bay City Rollers played at Glasgow during their tour during the spring of 1975. These two fans imagined that The Rollers would stay at the most expensive hotel, so they booked in there, paid £20 each for their stay, and were disappointed — the Rollers had not booked into that hotel at all! Perhaps, as fans, they should have known that the Rollers usually stay at a location 25 miles from their concerts' venues.

Another story about The Osmonds concerns their fans' initiative. One way of getting into a hotel if all the doors are guarded is to climb, so some Osmond fans whisked a ladder away from some property which was under repair, and were in the process of lining up the ladder against the hotel wall before someone spotted them. The ladder was long enough to reach the Osmonds' suite—some 60ft from the ground!

Some Rollers fans amazed London Transport travellers by carrying a 6ft by 5ft heart-shaped card across London to the home of the group's photographer. The card opened to reveal life-size cut-outs of a boy and girl kissing, dressed in tartan clothes similar to those of the Rollers.

Throughout the years, teen fans have always dressed in similar clothes to their stars, and some have gone to considerable lengths to do so. This was particularly noticeable during the glam-rock period, when audiences for Roxy Music and David Bowie concerts consisted of fans sporting hairstyles and make-up just like David's. Other fans have carefully outlined their eyes with black make-up, painted their cheekbones and temples scarlet, and added a gold circle on their foreheads. One person who managed to look uncannily like David Bowie had the name of Henry. Henry had David's brush-like hairstyle, high cheekbones and big wide eyes. He walked with the smoothness of his hero, and wore very high heels and a sparkling jacket. Adam Starr, a writer for *Mirabelle*, stated that he met Henry at a Mick Ronson concert, where he found Henry surrounded by stampeding fans requesting his autograph. Adam reported that Henry repeatedly denied that he was David but, nevertheless, he signed autograph books with a scrawl which read 'David Bowie'.

Recently a revival of rock 'n' roll has led to a re-emergence of tight trousers, leather jackets, greased-back hair and crepe-soled beetle-crusher shoes. The fans who dress in these clothes tend to be connected with such groups as Kilburn And The High Roads, Sha Na Na, Wild Angels, and Shakin' Stevens And The Sunsets.

In more recent times we have become accustomed to the Rollers and their fans dressed in tartan clothes. Surely no one can say that pop lacks colour and variety!

The Hit-makers

Critics of the pop scene say that very few artists ever last long at the top. In one sense they are right. There are no statistics showing how many artists fail to make one hit record during the year but in terms of records there is some evidence. During 1974, 4,034 records were issued and of these, 3,736 failed to gain a place in the Top 50 compiled by the British Market Research Bureau, the chart used by *Record Mirror*, *Sounds* and the music trade paper, *Music Week*.

There must be around 1,000 artists involved in making over 4,000 records and probably the figures are much higher. Add this kind of figure for each year of the 1970s—without even going back to the 1960s—and it's obvious that most pop artists never stay at the top.

However, the story isn't as depressing as the critics would have us believe, for on the pop scene there are a large number of artists who have had countless hits. Some of these artists started their hit trail in the 1950s! Two people come to mind straight away—Elvis Presley and Britain's own Cliff Richard.

Both Cliff and Elvis have over 50 Top 20 hits to their name in the singles listings and each has had many hit albums, though Elvis has done much better in this respect than Cliff has.

The first Elvis hit was in 1956. The title was *Heartbreak Hotel* and it was followed by *Blue Suede Shoes*. Elvis had an amazing number of hits each year in his early days.

The big pop artists of today rarely have even five hit records in one year—but in 1957 Elvis had nine! One year later Elvis had six hits within 12 months. Among other Elvis hit records have been *Teddy Bear*, *All Shook Up*, *Return To Sender* and *I Got Stung*.

And Elvis is still recording hit records! He had several big hits during 1974, not the least of which was the sale of some 800,000 album copies of a compilation of his biggest hits. One newspaper writer remarked that his 14-year-old daughter was busily decorating her bedroom with Elvis pictures

The Hit-makers

and posters.

Cliff's first big hit was *Move It* and among those to follow were *Livin' Doll*, *Bachelor Boy*, *Lucky Lips* and *The Day I Met Marie*. Cliff has always said that *The Day I Met Marie* is his favourite recording.

Cliff is now 34 years old and Elvis is 40. Both have made films and Cliff has appeared in several stage rôles—and neither of them look like fading yet!

Apart from Elvis and Cliff, there have been many hits from Duane Eddy, The Who, Stevie Wonder, Diana Ross—with or without The Supremes — The Hollies, The Rolling Stones, the four ex-Beatle members—Paul, John, George and Ringo—Andy Williams and Frank Sinatra. Frank's success has been mainly in recording albums. Until the end of 1973, he had had 33 albums in the British Top 10, as compiled in the excellent record book, *Rock File 2*, edited by Charlie Gillet.

In more recent years, Slade, the various Osmonds, Gary Glitter, Sweet, David Bowie, Mud and Marc Bolan have all had a considerable number of Top 20 hits.

The period of 1960-1973 saw The Beatles have more Number One album hits than anybody. They totalled 10. Second were The Rolling Stones with eight. In terms of Top 20 entries, Elvis was first with 37.

It's always interesting to speculate how many very popular artists of recent years will be making hits in 1980. When The Beatles had only been around for about two years there were people busily writing that they wouldn't last. How wrong they have been! Although the group is no longer together, and it did last many years, the four ex-members are still very successful as solo artists.

Will The Bay City Rollers, for example, still cause people to run down the aisles at concerts? Will Donny have become an entirely different type of artist by then? And what of Slade? We will know in years to come! Or will Elvis and Cliff still be around?

E.M.I. Records

cliff richard

Cliff was born in Lucknow, India, on 14 October 1940, and was therefore born under the sign of Libra. He was the eldest of four children and is the only son of Roger and Dorothy Webb. His father was a British engineer and his mother was, like Cliff, born in India, because her father was an officer in the British Army.

The Webb family came to Britain in 1948, after Harry Webb, as Cliff was christened, had received three years of schooling in India. When the family first arrived in Britain they went to live with Cliff's maternal grandmother in Carshalton. Life was hard for the Webb family at first but eventually they bought a house of their own in Cheshunt.

When Cliff was 11 years old, he failed his eleven-plus examination and went to Cheshunt Secondary Modern School. At school his surname, Webb, led to the nickname 'Spider', which he disliked. He did well at athletics, particularly with the javelin. At school he formed The Quintones, which was purely a singing harmony group with no musical backing. On leaving school, he started work in a factory.

He found himself in various groups and bought his first guitar. In July 1958 Cliff made his first record, which marked the start of his incredible British success. At that time, Cliff hadn't even started to perform on a professional basis.

Just before recording *Move It*, he became known as Cliff Richard. The musicians backing him at that time were called The Drifters, though on *Move It*, Hank Marvin did not play. Later The Drifters became known as The Shadows.

In Cliff's house the walls, even those of the toilet, are decorated with his many gold and silver discs. There are also cuttings and posters from his appearances at the London Palladium, and in pantomime, films and plays. His first major award was a gold disc for over 1,000,000 sales of *Livin' Doll*, a song which had come from his film *Serious Charge*. By 1975, Cliff had achieved six gold discs and no less than 23 silver records. Among his films have been *The Young Ones*, *Wonderful Life* and *Summer Holiday*. In the world of song he failed by just one vote to win the Eurovision Song Contest of 1968 with *Congratulations*.

Apart from concerts, recording work and travelling, much of his time is taken up with Christian work and he is very much involved with the Christian Arts Centre and Tear Fund, a charity which relieves famine, lack of medical facilities, and other difficulties in troubled countries.

Cliff still has personal ambitions and these would seem to lie in the desire to appear in a West End musical or stage presentation. He has stated that he would have liked the part of Jesus in *Godspell*, which was of course played by David Essex.

Cliff's discography would take pages but for anyone wishing to possess almost every Cliff single, there can be few, if any, better presentations than the one assembled by World Records. This includes eight exclusively compiled albums of hits by both Cliff and The Shadows, plus pictures of Cliff through the years, and a story booklet.

elton john

Elton was born in Pinner, Middlesex, on 25 March 1947 and was thus born under the star of Aries. He first played in a semi-professional group called Bluesology which had started on a semi-professional basis in 1964 in the Harrow, Middlesex, area. Elton played the organ in the group, which recorded its first disc in 1965. At that time Elton was known as Reg Dwight. Bluesology went through four different line-ups, but Elton left after the third. At one time the group backed Wilson Pickett on a British tour. At any rate, that was the idea—there was a disagreement and the band played only part of the tour.

He later toured with Major Lance, Patti LaBelle and Cindy Birdsong, who was later one of The Supremes. However, Elton wanted to sing and write songs, so he applied for a record company job. This was unfruitful and he found two companies who were *not* in need of his services!

Eventually he met Bernie Taupin and together they tried for success. They were signed on at DJM records as songwriters and were each paid £10 per week. Elton then left Bluesology and soon made his first solo album, *Empty Skies* and also a single, *Lady Samantha,* which had little immediate success. However, with help from Gus Dudgeon, Steve Brown and Paul Buckmaster, Elton and Bernie came up with the album *Elton John* and they were on the road to success at last.

Elton is continually on the move. He loves travelling, American radio stations and occasionally working as a DJ (as he did in Britain during Easter 1975). He collects paintings and antiques and, at one time, stuffed animals. One of his most treasured possessions is a toy koala bear. He tends the garden, enjoys playing squash and watching films, and has a house called Hercules very near to Windsor Castle. He has another residence on the American West Coast, to which he has shipped numerous paintings, since every wall of his English house was already overcrowded!

Elton has achieved tremendous success, even more so in America than in Britain. In the American publication *Calendar,* the writer Robert Hilburn stated, 'John's music (with Taupin's lyrics) is the rare blend of quality and excitement. It will be perfect for rock audiences who like to clap their hands and dance in the aisles because it is joyous, rhythmic music.'

Elton's Discography:

Singles

Lady Samantha—January 1969. *It's Me That You Need*—May 1969. *Border Song*—March 1970. *Rock And Roll Madonna*—June 1970. *Your Song*—January 1971. *Friends*—April 1971. *Rocket Man*—April 1972. *Honky Cat*—August 1972. *Crocodile Rock*—October 1972. *Daniel*—January 1973. *Saturday Night's Alright For Fighting*—June 1973. *Goodbye Yellow Brick Road* — November 1973. *Candle In The Wind* —February 1974. *Philadelphia Freedom*—March 1975.

Albums:

Empty Sky—1969. *Elton John*—1970. *Tumbleweed Connection* — 1970. *17.11.70*—1971. *Madman Across The Water*—1971 *Honky Chateau* — 1972. *Don't Shoot Me I'm Only The Piano Player*—1973. *Goodbye Yellow Brick Road*—1973. *Caribou*—1974. *Elton John's Greatest Hits*—1974. *Captain Fantastic And The Brown Dirt Cowboy*—1975. Film album: *Friends*—1971.

Solo singles: *I've Been Loving You*—1969. *Lady Samantha* — 1968. With Bluesology: *Come Back Baby, Mr Frantic*—1965. *Since I Met You Baby*—1968.

(At print, all Elton singles are available up to and including *Friends*—1971.)

Kate Simon Joseph Stevens

SPARKS

Remember Sparks' headline concert at Newcastle in November 1974? It was sensational and the audience went wild with excitement. Russell had some of his hair ripped out, and bass player Ian Hampton went to hospital with concussion. Sparks first achieved success here with singles such as *Amateur Hour* and *This Town Ain't Big Enough For Both Of Us*. However the Mael brothers—Russell and Ron—together with the rest of Sparks, returned to their native America for they desired success on both sides of the Atlantic. But they returned to Britain for another concert tour in November 1975, following a hit single, *Get In The Swing*, which was written by Ron.

gossip! gossip! gossip! gossip! gossip!

Long before he became a pop star David Essex played in several musicals and theatre productions. These included *The Fantasticks* and *Oh, Kay!* He also played cameo roles in films such as *All Coppers Are* and *Assault*.

****

Jim Gilstrap must be one of the few singers ever to audition with flu and pass all tests. This happened when he auditioned for the song *Swing Your Daddy*. Jim said that he was relieved when the producers also accepted his normal voice!

****

Rob Townshend of Family and Medicine Head fame says that he has one problem in life which will not go away. This is his height—he finds it very difficult at 5ft 4in. to find the right clothes. He says that when he tries 'off the peg' clothes they are usually a foot too long, jackets reach his knees, and trousers just trail along the floor!

****

Gary Glitter tells a very amusing story of how he once hung on to the lights during a concert. On this occasion Gary had spread his arms high and wide and to his amazement he found himself holding a couple of red hot bulbs. He had pulled them from their sockets, after forgetting how low the club roof was.

****

Rob of Mud is a keen yoga fan and he says that sometimes his mother's neighbours or callers at their home get a surprise. Over the fence they see someone apparently standing still the wrong way up, and they are completely amazed!

****

david essex

SUPERSTAR OF THE '70s

You will rarely see David at any pop party or reception. He prefers home comforts and the company of his wife Maureen and his daughter Verity. Their home contains many antiques which have been bought as a result of David's and Maureen's constant foraging round old and interesting shops. One item of particular interest in David's home is a large, old-fashioned juke-box which is full of discs from the 1950s and the rock 'n' roll era. This includes records by past stars such as Eddie Cochran, Fats Domino and Jerry Lee Lewis.

Verity has an enormous doll's house and many toys which David has brought back from America. Like David, she is also very fond of the two family dogs, Scruff and Rover. The two dogs often have quite a tussle! David loves animals and usually spends part of each day, when he is at home, taking the dogs for a good walk—a task usually assisted by Verity.

David and Maureen own a television but neither of them watch it very much. However, David does have an affection for the cinema, though he is not particularly keen on violent films. David prefers to talk rather than to watch television, and Maureen frequently invites friends to their home for musical evenings. Such occasions usually feature firstly a light meal with drinks, and the musical element follows.

Around the house David likes wearing sweaters, which are often old garments which he has bought at jumble sales. His trousers are casual and if he wears a sports jacket, it has usually had a time-honoured career. His shoes are usually flat-soled, and he does not appear to like shoes with high heels. Maureen wears very feminine clothes. She possesses old fur jackets and a collection of 1930s-style dresses, and she usually wears high-heeled shoes.

When David *does* appear amongst pop's fraternity, the event is usually a special one, and one which has occured without any particular plans having been made.

When David attended the Grammy Awards of 1975 his car had not arrived on time, and he and Maureen stood waiting on the pavement. John and Yoko Lennon were also staying at the same New York hotel, and they offered David and Maureen a lift in their car. John and David had not met before this chance meeting, but later in the evening the four went out together and had an enjoyable time.

On the same occasion David suddenly found himself amidst many of the stars whose music he had long admired. When he reached his dressing-room he found that a most interesting list of its occupants had been attached to the door. It read 'J Lennon, S Wonder, Wayne Jennings, P Simon . . .' It was certainly one of the most interesting dressing-rooms in the history of popular music! David was delighted.

David has very definite views on certain subjects and stubbornly refuses to change them. In some instances he is doubtless right to feel the way he does, and it is certainly not easy to cope with the endless pressures a pop star has to face. David's escape from these pressures is practically to go into hiding! He says that he must have time to write songs and he wants many hours with his family.

Even some of the people who are closest to his professional career have no idea where he lives now. This secrecy partly stems from his upset at having to move from his Primrose Hill area house in London, due to lack of privacy. For a long time David had cherished the thought of living somewhere central in London, in order to avoid delay and wasted time spent travelling into the city centre. His dream was short-lived, for crowds of people constantly gathered outside his front door. Some of them even began to peer through the letter-box, and many frequently rang the door-bell.

---

1 Name David's birthdate. **2** What was his father's job? **3** Name the secondary school he attended. **4** Name the first band in which he played drums. **5** Name the journalist who went to London's East End to hear David play. **6** Which football club attracted David? **7** David made two records with a girl singer. What was she called? **8** Name the venue of David's stage debut. **9** In which pantomime did David understudy Tommy Steele? **10** Where did David meet his wife Maureen? **11** Name the musical arranger with whom David works closely. **12** On which record label does David record? **13** Did *America* make the British Top 10? **14** Name the East End public house where David played with The Everons. **15** Name the London theatre at which David played for a week during his first major British concert tour.

Score 10 for attempting this quiz. Score 6 for each correct answer. All David fans should score at least 80. 70 and over Fairly good. **60** General pop fan mark.

10cc

1972 First record made for Jonathan King's UK record company.
1972 Their first single *Donna* enters charts.
1973 Third single, *Rubber Bullets* reaches Number One.
1973 Their first British tour. They record first album *10CC* at Strawberry Studios, Stockport.
1974 First tour of the United States. They appear in 107 cities.
1974 Second album issued called *Sheet Music*. It receives fantastic reception.
1975 They change record companies. They sign to Mercury for a reported fee of over £1,000,000.
1975 First album under new contract released called *The Original Sound Track*.

Status Quo

1966 First record under their original name, The Spectres.
1968 Changed name from Spectres to Status Quo.
1968 First Top Five single called *Pictures of Matchstick Men*.
1970 The group sign Colin Johnson as manager. Their record and fan decline is abated.
1972 First major sign of group's re-emergence with hit *Paper Plane* on a new company's label.
1973 First Number One album, *Piledriver*.
1974 Another Number One album, *Quo*.
1975 Third successive Number One album in Top 50 and called *On The Level*.

Report: Both groups show no signs of diminishing popularity. 10CC have a remarkable general age appeal and have achieved praise for all elements of their music, songs, vocal ability and musicianship.

Status Quo have some of pop's most fanatical and participant audiences. They have no special gimmicks but achieve success by ability to boogie.

David Bowie

1 Name the Japanese designer who has made many of David's clothes.

2 David played as a member of David Jones And The Lower Third, but of which other group was he once a member?

3 Which Canadian group once recorded three of David's songs?

4 What was his first job on leaving school?

5 David often worked with a drummer who played for Pentangle. What is this drummer's name?

6 Which film inspired David to write *Space Oddity*?

7 How long was he with the Lindsey Kemp Troupe?

8 What was his backing group called?

9 At what age did Mick Woodmansey start playing drums?

10 Which album depicts David with the pink zig zag on his face?

Score 10 points for each correct answer. If you're a Bowie fan you should score 90. Under 60 Never mind!

Queen

1 Name their first single.

2 What was the B side of *Seven Seas Of Rhye*?

3 Who produced their first album?

4 Brian May has a PhD degree in what subject?

5 Roger Meadows-Taylor has a BSc degree in which subject?

6 What was the name of the band which Brian and Roger once formed?

7 Name their record label.

8 On which album is the track *Ogre Battle* found?

9 Name the year of Freddie's birth.

10 From which bass players has John Deacon drawn much inspiration?

Score 10 points for each correct answer. As with the David Bowie quiz, no less than 90 for keen Queen fans. Under 70 Keep on reading!

Were you at Glasgow's Apollo Theatre, the opening venue of the Rollers 1975 tour? If you were, then you will remember the amazing scenes which made *Record Mirror* describe the event as 'Into The Eye Of A Hurricane'. There were also American journalists at the concert and, within days of the tartanmania scenes, over 300 American teen publications were reporting the incredible British response to The Bay City Rollers. One magazine reported that Tam and Les had wandered past a car showroom, gone in and promptly bought a vehicle costing about £10,000!

American promoter Sidney Bernstein, following the 1975 tour, promptly announced his booking of the Shea Stadium for a Bay City Rollers concert for the summer of 1975. The Shea Stadium is capable of seating an audience of 56,000 people, and has been the location of many famous pop concerts, including one by The Beatles.

The Rollers have not always known such success, however. In the past seven years or so of their existence, their first success came in June 1971 with a record called *Keep On Dancing*, which was produced by Jonathan King. It was not until March 1972 that their next record was released. This was called *We Can Make Magic*, and it was ignored by the British record buying public.

Some success did come the Rollers' way in September 1972 with the release of *Manana*, which won the Radio Luxembourg Grand Prix Song Contest that year. This song also reached Number One in Israel, but again the British record buying public turned its back on the Rollers and the song made no chart impression here.

So prior to the release of *Remember* near the end of 1973 the Rollers were disillusioned, lacking in confidence, and they later revealed that they were on the verge of giving up the search for success at that time. However, Tam Paton, their genial manager, spurred them on, despite the fact that they were tired of driving up and down Britain in a rather battered van. They had forgotten what good food tasted like—they were so used to eating slimy chips, overcooked sausages and half-cold bacon!

Admittedly the Rollers had a good fan following in smallish clubs throughout the country, but they badly wanted a hit record. During those grim times, their van wheel fell off and five girls had beaten them in a game of football—all in the space of a week!

The Rollers sat in Bell Record's offices where they gave interviews. Despite their troubles at that point in their careers, they were very friendly and their self-confidence was boosted by Tam Paton. Leslie talked about his liking for fast cars, and the fact that his father was a tailor. Eric mentioned that his home in Edinburgh was haunted, while Derek talked about his goldfish and said that he was building a 6ft by 3ft

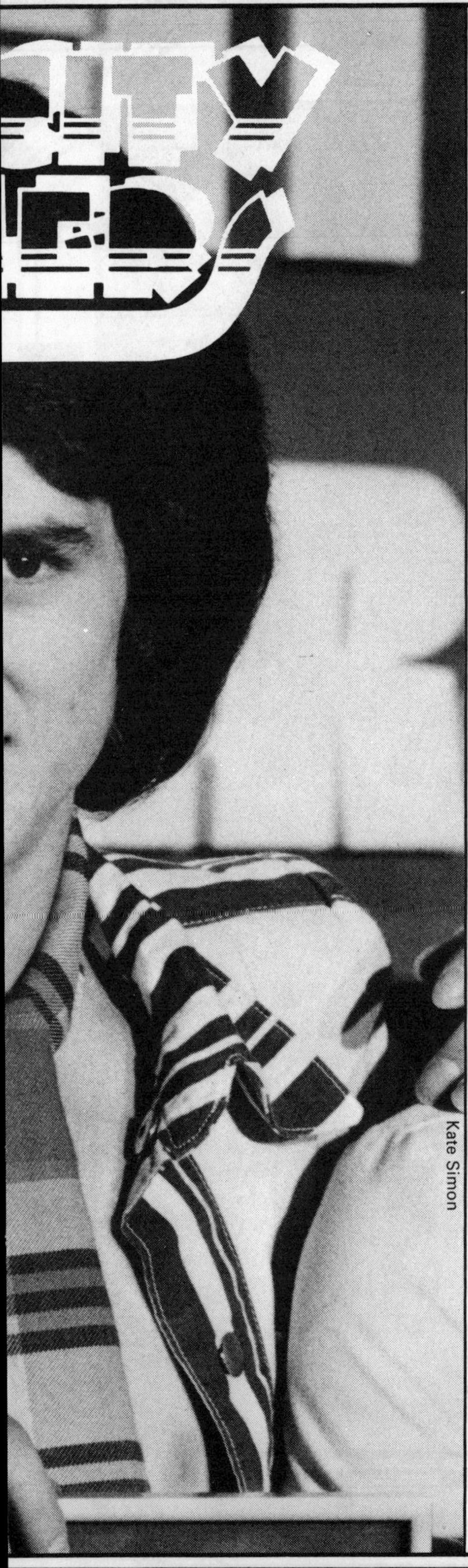

Kate Simon

tank for them. He also mentioned that his border collie, Jamie, was being looked after by his father while he was on tour.

Woody told of his swimming prowess and someone remarked that Woody had obtained a gold medal at the Olympics — a remark which made everyone laugh. Fishing and painting cropped up in Alan's conversation and someone said that the painting Alan was referring to was interior decorating! He also commented on his enjoyment of football and the fact that he really loved Edinburgh, though his visits home were few and far between.

However, their breakthrough was coming, although they were not aware of it at that time. *Remember* was a hit, followed by *Shang-A-Lang, Summerlove Sensation, Bye Bye Baby* and others. The Rollers' fan club gathered momentum and it now boasts membership figures which are larger than those for The Osmonds. Shortly afterwards the Rollers founded their own official boutique.

However, the Rollers seem to have changed very little since their huge success, and they have remained level-headed throughout the adulation of their fans. Perhaps the seemingly tight management of Tam has been a contributing factor, as he seems to have sheltered the boys from the pitfalls which fame has hoisted on to many pop people over the years. The Rollers can only look towards success from now on, although their American tour will not be an easy one for them, despite the advance publicity. If and when they pack the Shea Stadium in the summer of 1975, then we will know that the Rollers have triumphed.

Quiz

1 Who wrote *Marlina*? **2** Name Woody's star sign. **3** Which school did Derek and brother Alan attend? **4** Name Derek's first job. **5** Who wrote the Rollers' hit, *Shang-A-Lang*? **6** Name Tam's border collie dog which died at the age of 17. **7** Which is Les' favourite fish? **8** Which place near San Francisco is very important to the Rollers? **9** How old was Stuart when he joined the band? **10** Name the two Pilot members who have played in the Rollers.

Score 10 points for each correct answer. Roller fans should score 100. 80 and over Surprisingly high for non-Rollers fans, but good pop knowledge. **70** Fair. **60 and below** Moderate Roller knowledge.

Kate Simon

SLADE

Slade quiz

Slade fans should do well, but every pop fan stands a chance!

Noddy 1 In what year was he born? **2** What colour are his eyes? **3** Name the town where he was educated. **4** With whom does he write songs? **5** Name his star sign.

Jimmy 6 Name the exact place where he was born. **7** How tall is he? **8** At what age did he begin to play the violin? **9** With which orchestra did he play for some time? **10** Name two composers whom he highly respects.

Don 11 What is his complete name? **12** Of which boxing club was he once a member? **13** Did he play with Slade when they were known as Ambrose Slade? **14** Did he assist with the writing of *Look Wot You Dun*? **15** Which character did he play in *Flame*?

Dave 16 Where was he born? **17** Name his star sign. **18** Which member of his family has a doctorate in music? **19** What colour are his eyes? **20** In *Flame*, which character did he play?

General questions 21 Name their first single for Fontana. **22** What is the A side of *My Life Is Natural*? **23** Who became bass player of a group known as Nick And The Axemen? **24** During which month and year did Slade appear in a special concert called 'Fanfare For Europe'? **25** Which member of Slade was the first to cut his hair in their skinhead days?

Score four points for each correct answer. 92 and over Very good indeed, **78 and over** Quite good, particularly if you score 88, **Under 78** Providing you have not scored below 52, the result is fair, but means much more Slade-work is needed!

Gary Glitter

The other evening I was walking towards London's Notting Hill Gate area when I heard someone busily tooting his horn at me. The sound came from a rather smart Mercedes car on the far side of the road, so I walked across to investigate. The automatic window was lowered. A rather gorgeous looking girl was sitting in the car, but at her side was Gary Glitter. He shouted out a greeting and we had quite a chat before Gary finally moved off to his planned destination.

I tell this story as an illustration of how friendly and down-to-earth Gary is, when compared to those snobbish, patronising pop stars who act in an off-handed manner.

Gary is certainly one of the best stars to interview for teen magazines. Nothing is too much trouble for him, and he always has amusing stories and memories to relate. Unlike some pop stars, Gary has had to work hard for his fame and fortune, and no doubt this long struggle for success is the reason for Gary's obvious dedication to his many fans. This dedication and care is reflected in his shows, which cost him a great deal of money. For example, at one show motorbikes raced on to the stage, and after circling round their riders lined them up and made the bikes 'rev' in time to the Glitter Band's beat in the background. Gary arrived on a motorbike as a pillion passenger and shouted the lines 'I'm The Leader Of The Gang I Am!'

Once Gary was a singer known as Paul Raven, but he had very little success, and was obscured by stars such as The Beatles, The Hollies and Frankie Vaughan. He learnt his trade by singing in small clubs in both Britain and Germany—the latter being the country where The Beatles found early acclaim.

It was not until 1972 that Gary found some real success. He stunned everyone by appearing with a new name, Gary Glitter, and with clothes to match! The papers claimed that he spent £300 a week on clothes and everyone started to talk about his shining sequins, his eye make-up and the enormous stacked heels on his shoes. He reduced his weight from 13st to 11st 5lb in two months, and he therefore achieved the ideal weight for his height of 5ft 8in. He told *The Sun* newspaper, 'Shiny gear looks daft clinging to a fatty!'

He knew he was moving towards stardom when girls clambered onto the stage during his act and his jackets, which later cost several hundred pounds each, were regularly torn to pieces. He also saw positive signs of stardom in the sales of his records. The first was *Rock 'n' Roll, Parts 1 And 2*. However, it did take four months to break into the charts. The records which followed hardly wasted any time at all before arriving in the Top Five — records such as *Do You Wanna Touch Me*, *Always Yours* and *I Love You Love Me Love*.

Gary was very worried at the end of 1974 because he was faced with a throat operation. His fears of a serious disease were unfounded, as he later discovered from hospital reports, but he did require a minor operation. However, the box-office reaction to his first film *Remember Me This Way* soon cheered him up!

Joseph Stevens

SMONDS

From the past to the present

Where does one start with The Osmonds? When writer Peter Jones told the story of The Osmonds in *Record Mirror*, he went beyond the wedding of Olive and George, which took place in Ogden, Utah, on 1 December 1944. He related the story of Olive Davis, an 18-year-old secretary, who was one day cutting stencils which would form American army training manuals. Into the room came 26-year-old George Virl Osmond, and it was love at first sight!

The MGM Records press release begins The Osmonds' story with the Andy Williams and Jerry Lewis television shows on which the brothers appeared. At that time there were four Osmond brothers performing, but by 1969 the fifth member, Donny, had joined. Prior to this he had made only occasional appearances. Nowadays, however, there are seven Osmonds, of course—Alan, Jay, Merrill, Donny, Wayne, Jimmy and Marie.

During one of their British visits Donny was asked why he records so many old songs such as *Puppy Love* and *When I Fall In Love*. Donny said that these songs described his feelings very accurately, and he was sure that the same was true of other teenagers. He added that old songs were enjoyable to listen to and, unless one had older brothers and sisters, they probably seemed like new songs to his generation.

Donny stated that The Osmonds do see all the presents which are sent to them by fans, and he reads every book on electronics which is sent to him. Electronics are his hobby and in his bedroom he has innumerable electrical gadgets. One of these is a device which enables his bed to revolve! He also said that The Osmonds have a special store for all gifts which are sent to them by fans, in addition to a library for the many books which they receive on a wide variety of subjects.

During another visit to Britain they rehearsed and presented a series of television shows which ran for one week. The Osmonds impressed the shows' production crew with their work rate, and they also took great care to ensure that everything was presented in the best possible way.

Many people were impressed by the friendliness of all The Osmonds, who threw a party for everyone who had been involved with their visit. At this party they all spent several hours meeting and talking to everyone.

As with all their visits, the place where they actually stayed was kept a closely-guarded secret. However, several London press photographers did find out the location and appeared at the front door of the large house which had been rented for the duration of the visit—much to the amazement of The Osmonds!

Fortunately, The Osmonds do not appear to get bored by having to remain indoors, and pursue many interests instead. For example, during that particular visit, Donny busily delved into the subject of Egyptian archaeology, while Alan and Merrill's wives, Suzanne and Mary, discussed the shops and landmarks in London which they visited each day.

Donny also spent much of his free time changing two ordinary pianos into what he called his 'magic' ones. He likes playing rock 'n' roll and even some Dixie-style music. Often his brothers and the girls drifted along to where he was playing his music, and hummed or sang along with him. Table football was another popular recreation, although Jimmy preferred to go outside and kick a real football around.

For part of that visit they began to eat typically British foods such as bacon and eggs, but as the week wore on the British foods were abandoned in favour of more typical American dishes such as maple syrup pancakes. They particularly enjoy apple and blackberry pies and lemon meringues. Fresh fruit is also very popular with The Osmonds, but they never eat very sweet foods.

The Osmonds have been back to Britain during 1975 and in recording terms, Donny, Jimmy and Marie have all had solo albums released. Donny has recorded with Marie, and of course with all his brothers. Maureen Street, their British fan club secretary, has said that their fans are growing up with them so she fully expects that when Donny is 30 years old he, like Cliff Richard, will have taken his fans with him and will doubtless have found fans from the next generation!

QUIZ *Rather a hard one unless you are an enthusiastic Osmond fan. Nevertheless, try it and see where you stand!*

1 In what year was Jimmy born? **2** State the year when the brothers had their own TV show in America. **3** What is Donny's full name? **4** How many gold records did The Osmonds receive between September 1971 and September 1972? **5** Where did Mary Carisson teach prior to her marriage? **6** Who was Marie named after? **7** Name Jay's favourite colours. **8** The food of which country is loved by Wayne? **9** What was Alan's wife's surname before she married? **10** What was the B side of Marie's first single, *Paper Roses?* **11** What did Suzanne's bridesmaids wear at her wedding? **12** Which two names do Donny's brothers use as nicknames for him? **13** What is the name of the American drink made from milk powder and ice cream soda which is enjoyed by Donny? **14** Where was Donny born? **15** What are Marie's two favourite foods?

Score 1 point for each correct answer.

15: Good. You must be a fan club member; **12-14:** Pretty good, and very good if you're not a fan; **8-11:** Fair; **Under 8:** If you're a fan, join the fan club quickly! You need their help!

Kate Simon

QUICK QUIZZES

Elton John 1 In which year was he born? 2 Name his favourite football team. 3 What is his real name? 4 Name his lyricist. 5 What was his original hair colour? 6 Has he ever appeared on a Royal Command Performance?

DJs 7 What is Stewpot's real name? 8 Where was Tony Blackburn born? 9 For which profession did Stuart Henry train? 10 How many 'O' levels did Noel Edmonds obtain?

Gilbert O'Sullivan 11 In which year was he born? 12 How many children are there in his immediate family? 13 Is he left - or right-handed? 14 What is his manager's name?

Lynsey de Paul 15 How old is she? 16 Where was she born? 17 How tall is she? 18 Which college did she attend? 19 With which hit artist does she often write songs?

Kenny 20 How many members are there in the group? 21 Which subject did Chris Redburn once study? 22 What was their first hit? 23 What is their drummer called? 24 Name their songwriters.

Pilot 25 From which country do they come? 26 Were any of them ever with The Bay City Rollers? 27 Name their drummer. 28 What is the title of their second hit?

Peter Shelley 29 For which artist does Peter write and produce songs? 30 Name the title of his animal record! 31 With which once-famous rock 'n' roll star does he work? (This artist has a son called Ricky.) 32 Name his record company label.

Mike McGear 33 Name his brother. 34 Where is he from? 35 With which group has he been associated? 36 Has he written a children's book?

The Glitter Band 37 Which member left the group during 1974? 38 Which famous star do they back? 39 Name their second album. 40 Which group member wrote *The Tears I Cried*?

The Wombles 41 Name the lady who writes the Womble books. 42 Name their musical arranger. 43 Which was the first Womble to hit the streets? 44 Name The Wombles' classically-based disc. 45 Name the most intelligent Womble.

Take 5 marks as a bonus for answering these questions. 2 marks for each correct answer and then you will have your total out of 100.

90-100 First class. You have a wide knowledge of pop. **75-89** You're coming on but maybe you just listen to the few people you like instead of observing everyone. **60-74** Not bad but you could do better. Keep reading the pop magazines. **Under 44** Try one of the other quizzes!

Fashion

Back in the late 1940s men wore zoot suits, which were suits with wide, padded shoulders, drape jackets and wide trousers. When the men were thus attired, they went to jazz clubs.

In the early 1950s the Teddy boys, Elvis Presley and rock 'n' roll arrived. The dance which was popular then was jiving, which was extremely energetic and aggressive. The Teddy boys wore long, pointed 'winkle-picker' shoes and fluorescent, luminous socks which glowed in the dark or reflected the lights in clubs. Trousers were narrow 'drain-pipes', ties were like boot-laces, and shirts had frills. Hair was cut short, except for fringes which were swept back into quiffs, and liberally plastered with hair cream. Sideburns reached down to the chin. The 'Teds' wore flashy waistcoats, and carried all their items of clothing to extremes.

Girls in the 1950s wore short, pencil-slim skirts, and fishnet stockings held up by suspenders. Some wore skirts which were loose and wide and when the energetic jiving required the girl to be swung into the air, she showed endless layers of white net petticoat. The girls often wore tight sweaters and usually wide cinch belts. Nails and lips were painted a vivid red, and hairstyles were backcombed into a 'beehive', or pulled back into a ponytail.

Music in the 1950s came from artists such as Fats Domino, Eddie Cochran, Jerry Lee Lewis, Bill Haley, Larry Williams and Charlie Gracie. The 1950s

Syndication International

Syndication International

was a period when boys remained 'cool', and girls waited for the invitation to dance.

The Rockers arrived somewhere around the late 1950s and they lived for their motorbikes and wore leather clothing, covered with countless studs and coloured transfers. Their bikes were made for high speed and Rockers frequently competed to do the 'ton', which was to reach 100 m.p.h. on a motorbike. Rockers were usually to be found in certain motorway cafés, and their music, like the Teddy boys, was rock 'n' roll.

There were also the Beats who grew their hair to shoulder-length—something regarded as outrageous and obnoxious by many people in the 1950s. Beats came mainly from grammar schools, whereas Rockers almost always tended to be ex-secondary modern pupils. Beats were more interested in literature than creating a dance form or idolising pop stars.

The late 1950s and early 1960s saw the folk movement boom, and people became concerned about world politics and, in particular, the effects of nuclear bomb testing. Musicians who were involved with this movement were Bob Dylan, Joan Baez and Tom Paxton. In Britain there were folk singers such as Ewan McColl and A. L. Lloyd.

Clothes during that time were simple, and both sexes wore jeans and black sweaters, and sometimes suede jackets.

The Mods arrived in the early to mid-1960s, and boys were still 'cool', and rode scooters. They often had fights with Rockers, and some of their story has been immortalised in the LP *Quadrophenia* by The Who. Male Mods raced around in what were called Scooter Kid's Parkas. Trousers were hipsters and were sometimes very tight indeed. Belts were small—

Syndication International

around an inch in width—and jackets and suits were tailored. Shirts were a different colour from their collars, and rollneck sweaters were fashionable.

Among the stars of the mid-1960s were The Who, The Beatles, The Searchers, Billy J. Kramer And The Dakotas, Gerry And The Pacemakers, and Billy Fury. The Who were regarded as the Mods' group.

By 1967 girl pop fans were wearing suits with straight trousers topped with different styled jackets, which often had a frocked effect and large, flat lapels. The suits were adorned with big bold brass buttons, and herringbone wool was in vogue. Men copied ideas from the girls at that time! They wore chain-fronted shoes, very long overcoats, and crew-neck jumpers. Guards' jackets were very fashionable, but people were warned that decorative buttons had to be removed. Many people began to wear capes which had richly-coloured linings, and denim was the fashionable material for raincoats. When the guys went to clubs they wore candy-striped shirts, antique glasses, ties which were knotted to look like cravats, long jackets with two

Syndication International

vents, and straight-cut trousers. Boots were in Regency style with wide leather belts round the soles in contrasting colours to the shoes.

The prices of clothes in 1968? Suits cost £15, shoes just under £5, ties £1.50, and shirts £3.25. Girls' trousers were about £4.75 and jackets cost £7. Clinging sweaters for girls, known as 'skinny rib' jumpers, which accentuated the female contours cost £1.60 and a cord suit used to cost about £13.

The late 1960s also saw Flower Power, with gentle songs of love and peace from the American West Coast from groups such as The Mamas And Papas, and also more violent sounds from such groups as Jefferson Airplane and Grateful Dead. There was also a host of groups with colourful names such as Mint Taboo, Pipe Joint Compound, Colossal Pomegranate, Angels Own Social Grace And Deliverance Band, and Peter Wheat And The Bread Men.

Flower Power people wore exotic colours and usually attempted extravagant make-up of their faces and bare bodies! Bells jingled from bodies or wrists and the attempt was made to communicate peace and general goodwill. Drug-taking became fashionable.

There were also Hippies, and religious groups with their heads completely shaved apart from a little tail of hair down the back. People wore old denim jackets and old jeans, which often had wide, flared trousers. Old clothes became very fashionable and people scoured old clothes shops for garments from another generation.

Satin became popularised in the 1970s by stars such as Marc Bolan and Rod Stewart, and glitter came with Gary. The 1970s have brought fashions for styles from the 1920s and 1930s, so pencil-slim skirts and high-heeled shoes with slim bases have come into vogue.

Glam-rock has come and gone and, amidst all these other styles, there have also been mini, midi and maxi skirts, plus hot pants, skirts slit up the side, and dresses buttoned down the front. There has been a cult of the boyish figure, typified at one time by Twiggy. Height has been part of the long flared trouser look with thighs and waists clutched, so many have found it necessary to wear very high heeled shoes (including boys)! Unisex was the rage at one time, and is still with us in many instances, for sexual distinction has in some ways become blurred.

All these fashions have become mixed up with the music and dances of the time. Whether fashion is dictated, or whether some fans set the pace and manufacturers then quickly copy will always remain debatable. However, designers such as Mary Quant and Barbara Hulanicki (Biba) have had tremendous influence from the top end of the fashion business.

What will come next is anybody's guess, though whatever may be fashionable in the shops, there will always be those people in slightly exclusive circles who create their own styles, or copy the trimmings and dress of their favourite star.

Such was the case when the girl trio called Labelle visited Britain in 1975. The three members of the group—Nona, Sarah and Patti—came dressed in futuristic clothes of a space age. Advance television showings of the group encouraged some of their audience to come bedecked in colourful clothes of similar styles.

Nona wore a tight-fitting silver space suit with high platform boots. Sarah wore a loose-fitting silver gown plus a large silver sunhat. Patti had her hair adorned with a large silver streak and she was completely covered in sparkling material.

In the second half of their show the most incredible stage appearance was effected. At the back of the stage there was a platform with steps. Sarah was to be seen emerging at the top of the stairs, completely covered in black feathers from her head-dress to her long cape.

When she turned and walked down the stairs towards the audience, attention turned to Nona. She appeared in a white space suit with special studs around her breasts and abdomen region. She, too, wore a large feathered head-dress and studded platform boots. Patti was not on the steps as the other two had been—she arrived by being lowered from the ceiling!

She was dressed in a long orange feathered cape which was removed, when she reached the stage, to reveal a copper-coloured space suit.

Could this be the shape of things to come?

C.B.S. Records

QUICK QUIZZES

This quiz is much harder because it involves artists who are not often in the Top 50, although their albums often sell very well.

Sparks **1** Name their first UK album. **2** Which member has a very stony facial expression? **3** Name their old US hit single. **4** What were they called originally?

Clifford T. Ward **5** Where was he born? **6** Name his first Charisma album. **7** Name his first successful hit single. **8** How many tracks are there on *Escalator*?

Little Feat **9** Name their leader. **10** When was their first album released? **11** Name the group's first LP. **12** Who wrote *On Your Way Down*?

Supertramp **13** Name their third album. **14** Name the producer of their third album. **15** Name the major writers in the group. **16** What is the name of the bass player?

Al Stewart **17** Name his album with the title connected with bed-sit land. **18** Is he British? **19** What is the name of his producer, who won a Grammy award for helping Pink Floyd? **20** Name his album with a 'fruity' title!

The Doobie Brothers **21** What was the title of their first UK hit single? **22** Name their album with the word 'street' in the title. **23** Name their third album. **24** Name their two drummers. **25** Which disc jockey used *Listen To The Music* as his programme signature tune?

Score 4 points for each correct answer. **85-100** Very good indeed. **75-84** Not bad. **60-74** Widen your musical interests! **Under 60** You must be a Bay City Rollers fan!

pop reporter

How do you become a pop reporter?
Most people who work on weekly pop papers or teen magazines were originally journalists. Most of them have worked on a small town or large city newspaper, while a few have worked on student magazines.

The ages of pop reporters vary from about 16 years to people in their thirties and sometimes older. If you write to an editor always enclose some cuttings, however small, from a magazine or paper which has published any articles you have written.

What musical qualifications do you need?
Hardly any papers ask for any, but when they are choosing a person for a job they may well prefer someone who plays, or has played, in a band. Basically they want someone who knows about the present music scene. Remember—you will have to write about a wide range of artists and not just your personal favourites. Obviously it's no good liking Osmond music and applying to a heavy rock paper!

Is it hard work?
The job is often an 18 hours a day one, so you need patience and boundless energy. Office hours may be 9.30 to 5.30, but there are also evening gigs and rushes to the airport to meet stars. Sometimes you have to fly abroad to concerts, and linger around clubs for possible stories.

Are girls employed?
Boys outnumber girls on the weekly pop papers, but the opposite is true of the teen magazines. Check the names of staff listed in the weekly pop papers and you will see which ones favour girls.

Is the money good?
Payment is laid down by the trade unions concerned, but some firms where there is no trade union have their own rates of pay. Wages can be very low if you are engaged to take messages or sort photographs, but even the smallest job can be a stepping stone to something better. An average rate of pay might be around £45 a week, with fairly good expenses in addition.

What do you do during your week?
Work hard! I try to make sure that I know of most events which are happening in the pop world—which can mean anything from a group splitting up to a star suddenly arriving in London. I read all the musical papers and magazines and most, if not all, of the teen papers. I also read the trade papers, which are published for people who work in recording studios and record companies, for music publishers and record shop owners—in fact, practically everyone who makes a living from pop.

I listen to most albums and singles which are released each week, and I go to record receptions, which are usually held when an artist or group has released a new album. Sometimes these are held when a foreign pop star visits this country. I also attend concerts and go to some clubs.

Each week I interview quite a few artists. At interviews, I use a form of shorthand, and on other occasions I use a tape machine. The best machines are those with built-in microphones, because with these machines you can concentrate on talking, without having to worry about holding the microphone or knocking it over.

How do you translate the interview into the finished article?
This depends on the kind of magazine for which you are writing. Some magazines or papers prefer to include personal stories from the artists, while other periodicals prefer to print much more musical and autobiographical material.

I read through my notes or listen to the taped material and jot down quotes which I think are particularly good. I then decide how an article should begin and proceed to write up the interview.

When the article is written it is given to a sub-editor, who corrects bad grammar and lazy expression, and in some cases changes the writer's copy to suit the general style of the paper.

Do you enjoy listening to all the records you receive?
After listening to pop and rock for years you seem to develop a sixth sense as to what may or may not be successful.

I often play albums as background music when I am doing something else, and I find that if I become aware of the music, then the disc must contain a special element. I do pay more attention when I am reviewing records, since I am being paid to listen for the purpose of writing about them for a pop paper.

Who have you enjoyed meeting most?
That's a difficult question to answer, as there is more to being a journalist than instinctively liking someone as an artist, because the reason you are meeting stars is to find out something interesting to write about them. There are many people with whom I have enjoyed talking, such as Cliff Richard, David Essex, Olivia Newton-John, Mike Batt, Clifford T. Ward, and Joan Baez.

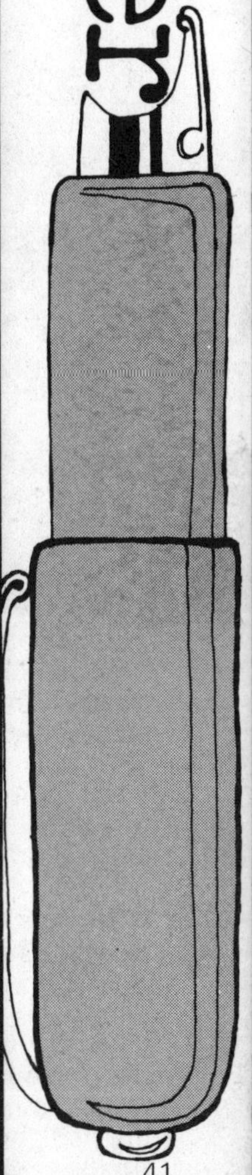

★ PAUL & WINGS ★

You probably know all about Paul's background, from his Liverpool schooldays, to his time with The Beatles, then his career as a solo artist, and now his present successes with Wings. When he was a member of The Beatles, he used to write songs with John Lennon, but he has written songs on his own for Wings such as *C Moon, Hi Hi Hi, Band On The Run,* and *Listen To What The Man Says.*

Linda comes from Scarsdale, New York, and music has always been a part of her life, as stars used to visit her home when she was a child. She said that she was forced to learn how to play the piano when she was young, but when she was older she used to listen to Chuck Berry, Buddy Holly and Jerry Lee Lewis.

She studied at an American university, then married but was later divorced. She settled in Arizona with her daughter Heather, but went back to New York to work on a magazine there, for she was a good photographer. It was through her work in photography that she met Paul. She later married him, and Paul, Linda and Heather moved to Britain where Paul has a London house and a Scottish farm. The McCartneys now have two children of their own—Stella and Mary.

Apart from their music and their country life in Scotland, Paul and Linda enjoy lavish events. In 1975 they had a party on the *Queen Mary,* and their early summer album *Venus And Mars Are Alright Tonight*, provided the theme for the party. Everything was decorated in red and yellow, and the ballroom was decorated in New Orleans style, recalling Paul and Linda's visit to that city's Mardi Gras. Many pop stars attended the party, which was a huge success—obviously the McCartneys do everything in style!

four of britain's best

They're called **Mud,** and they've been playing together as a group for years. In February 1974, after seven years or more, Mud hit the big time. Their first chart entry was *Crazy,* followed soon after by *Hypnosis.* They owed much to songwriters Nicky Chinn and Mike Chapman and the people of RAK record company at that time. Since then they've had nothing but success, although they no longer work with Chinn and Chapman. Their late 1974 hit, *Lonely This Christmas,* sold over 800,000 copies, which shows the popularity of this group.

Alvin Stardust was once known as Shane Fenton, but he found fame as Alvin with a Number Two smash hit called *My Coo-Ca Choo.* He works with producer and writer Peter Shelley, and during 1974 he sold more records than any other male solo artist. He loves his life in the musical world, but he once said that he would like a career as a Royal Canadian Mounted Police officer!

The Rubettes were once a group who helped others to make the hits. They went on tour with Barry Blue but by the end of the tour they were hit-makers in their own right, because their record *Sugar Baby Love* became a world-wide smash hit. Their critics said that they wouldn't last but, as they stated on their 1975 album, *We Can Do It.* The hits have continued and the group have set their hearts on having a success in America. One of their 'trademarks' is wearing suits and caps. Success came so quickly for them that, in order to make their first appearance on *Top Of The Pops,* they had to rush out and buy suits. Girls at their record company added the final items of tailoring!

The Glitter Band back Gary but they said that they could make hits on their own as well. They were right—they have had a string of hits. As one magazine stated 'All that glitters isn't Gary'. However, in the spring of 1975 they said that their glitter image would be phased out. John Rossall left to go solo in 1974, and the group did not add another member. Their ambition is well summed up by Gerry's statement—'I discovered my true vocation—as a Glitterman!'

1

2

3

4

Polydor Records Ltd.

POP CHASER

Find some friends, a counter each and a dice anc you're almost away on *pop chaser*!

Choose which group or singer you want to be, anc live a chart chase with your opponents. Play lots o

127	128	129 Steady your nerves. **Forward to 132.**	130 Good response from audience. **Forward to 133.**	131 Riot at concert because you didn't play old hits, only new ones. **Back to 91.**	132	133
126	125	124	123 Short spell of radio and TV promotion. **Onwards to 132!**	122	121 Shop deliveries hindered. **Back to 113.**	120 Quiet but effective sales. **Forward to 128**
99	100 You're too confident. **Back to 83** as you're playing bad gigs.	101	102	103	104	105
98	97	96	95	94	93 You're accused of making naughty records. **Back to 87.**	92
71 Sickness hits group or solo artist. **Back to 59.**	72	73	74	75	76	77
70	69	68	67 Take a rest and stay put!	66 Tipped for top by everybody. **On to 99.**	65	64 Trailer carryin thousands of you discs overturns. **Back to 40.**
43 Recording problems hold up record. **Back to 32.**	44	45 Group or solo singer refused entry back to Britain. **Back to 8.**	46	47	48	49 Lovely concer tour. **Onwards 2 places!**
42	41	40	39 You appear on *Top Of The Pops.* **Forward 20.**	38	37 Gig cancelled, so some record sales lost. **Back 5.**	36
15	16	17	18	19 Rude reviews of disc. **Back 11.**	20	21
14	13	12	11 The discos like your record. **Forward 17.**	10 Lead singer in hospital. **Back 9.**	9 Plenty of promotion. **Forward 12.**	8

games and keep a tally of how your group or singer fares! If it gets too slow, then throw two dice.

You can only go out of the game if you land exactly on 140. If you are over then go back the number above 140 which you have thrown. For example, if you land on 139 and you throw a 6, go forward one place to 140, then back to 135 for the 5 too many that you've thrown.

4	135 **Back to 126** because your disc was cut at ending of *Top Of The Pops.*	136 **Back to 133** owing to strain and stress.	137 Writ served on you. **Take a trip to 46.**	138 American tour. and recording dates cancelled. Agent sues. **Back to 30.**	139	140 Top of the pops!
9 Copyright ections so ord withdrawn. **ck to 75.**	118	117	116	115	114	113
6 **Go to 108** and what that says!	107 Stop here. Momentary lull in fortunes.	108 **On to 111.** Well, it's better than the other way!	109	110	111	112 Extra push by record company. **Progress to 124.**
	90 Nice progress over past days. **Forward to 105.**	89	88	87	86 National power cuts affect attendances. **Back to 69.**	85
	79 Manager from your past sues you. Court order halts all records. **Back to 36.**	80 Sales progressing. **Forward to 98.**	81 Fairly good progress. **Forward 11.**	82	83	84
Noel says your ord's great. **wards to 91.**	02	61	60 Shops cautious with your new disc. **Back to 51.**	59	58 Local radio station turns down disc. **Back to 42.**	57
Records delayed elease—doesn't chart chances. **ck to 38.**	51	52 Good sales this week. **Go forward 11.**	53	54	55	56 Radio One play for disc. **Forward to 84.**
Fog prevents reaching an ortant TV earance. **Go k 10.**	34 Good reviews in pop paper. **Forward 10.**	33 20,000 albums sold on first day of sale. **Forward 29 places.**	32	31	30	29
	23	24	25	26	27	28
	6	5 The DJs love your group. **Forward 17 places.**	4	3	2	1

Girls

Girls by Moments And Whatnauts was a big hit in Britain and America during 1975. It talked of girls superfine, mighty fine and all things nice.
Yet if girls are super, why do they have such a hard task to prove themselves in the British record charts? Perhaps it has something to do with the rôle of women in British society. Maybe their songs aren't strong enough. However, in America girl singers have always done well, so the reason why girls rarely hold chart places in Britain is a complete mystery. Even more strange is the way in which many fine British girl artists are ignored by the general British record-buying public. Some of these artists include Lesley Duncan, Juliet Lawson, Kiki Dee, Elkie Brooks, Madeline Bell, Sandy Denny and Lyn Paul.

In a list in *Record Mirror* of top-selling girl singers, based on chart appearance, which was compiled at the end of 1974, 10 names could not be found. However, a dramatic change occurred during April 1975, when 17 girl soloists or groups made the Top 50 during the space of a few weeks. Many of these names were new to Britain—such as reggae singer Susan Cadogan; soul singer Minnie Ripperton; and a popular country artist, Tammy Wynette.
British girls who have managed to break through and get real attention include Lena Zavaroni, Olivia Newton-John, Lulu, Lynsey de Paul and Cilla Black. Perhaps Suzi Quatro should be included, since success in Britain came for her when she became a resident over here.

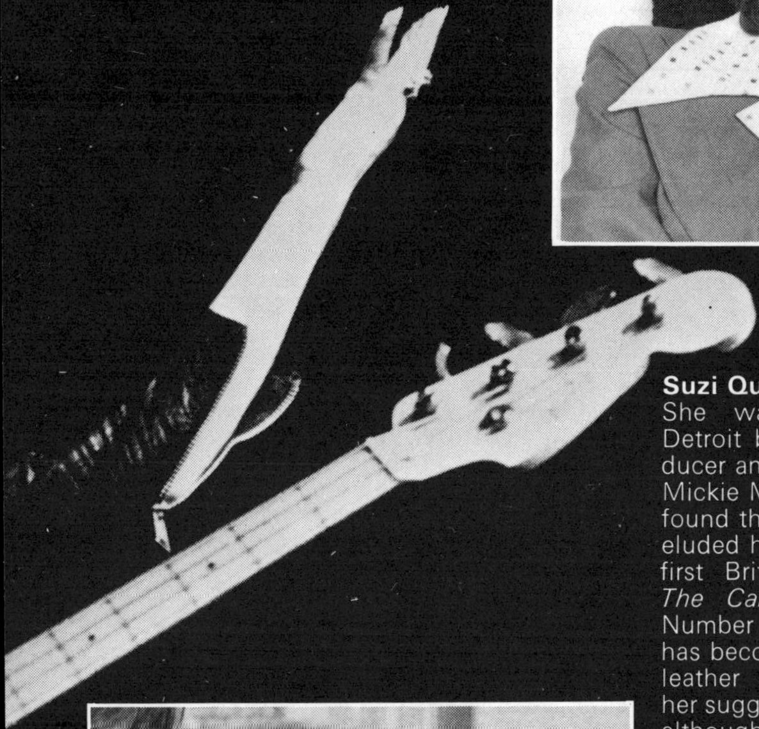

Kate Simon

Suzi Quatro
She was discovered in Detroit by the record producer and company owner, Mickie Most. In Britain she found the success that had eluded her for so long. Her first British hit was *Can The Can* which reached Number One in 1973. Suzi has become famous for her leather stage outfits and her suggested tough image, although she says that she has a very soft streak in her nature. She has a sister called Patti who sings with the all-female group, Fanny.

Lynsey de Paul
Lynsey makes mad jokes and is very pleased with her singing and songwriting career. She is clever at graphic design, and studied this subject at Hornsey College of Art in North London. Her first hit record was *Sugar Me*, although she had already written several hit songs for other artists before that. One hit which gave Lynsey particular pleasure was the theme music for the television programme *No Honestly*. She also writes hits with Barry Blue.

Olivia Newton-John
Olivia is Australian, but has spent most of her life in Britain. However, because she achieved incredible success in America, she has now set up home there and has an American manager. Her first solo hit in Britain was *If Not For You* in 1971. In America she constantly tops the record charts. It's a shame that her fame in Britain is nowhere near that of her success in America.

Kiki Dee
She comes from Bradford and spent years providing a backing voice for many pop stars. Until she signed with Elton John's record company, Rocket Records, personal fame escaped her. However, the song *Amoureuse* changed all that, for it was with that song that she made her first chart entry. Her vocal variety was shown in another hit, *I've Got The Music In Me*.

david fas

David Cassidy left the music scene after his world tour during the early summer of 1974. He decided to reconsider his career and to find out what he really wanted from his life. He also wanted to decide whether he still wanted music and show business to feature strongly in his future.

Indeed, no David singles, apart from a re-issue of *White Christmas* with The Partridge Family, were issued after the end of that tour, and the only David album which has been released since his 'retirement' has been a compilation of his greatest hits.

However, on 21 February 1975 an important communication for all David Cassidy fans was released by a different record company from the one with which he has been associated for some years.

This newsletter is printed on the next page, and from this you will gather why it could be risky 'remembering' David, since by the time this volume reaches you, he might be back in the spotlight once more. Perhaps he will return with a new style and a new sound, and this is quite likely because he has been recording with ex-Beach Boy, Bruce Johnston, as his producer.

However, some memories perhaps! David's first tour of Britain was not long after a television writers' strike in Hollywood, which had delayed the production of The Partridge Family television series. The strike had given him some time off. He announced on this occasion 'I've wanted some time to think. I ask myself, what do I want to do? Where do I want to go? I don't have the answers yet, but maybe I will soon.' He also said that he really wanted to widen his musical horizons, and he felt that he had managed to do so on his new album of the time *Dreams, Nothing More Than Wishes*. He was particularly proud of one track on that album—*Bali Hi*. He said that *Bali Hi* 'comes from the show *South Pacific*. I'm too young to have seen the stage-show, but I've seen the film.' David also remarked that his father often hummed that tune in his bath, so David could remember it from his childhood days.

By the time of his British visit during the summer of 1974 he had made up his mind to semi-retire from show business. At that time, he looked very tired and appeared to be under stress. In fact, he had taken a day's holiday during his visit in order to spend some quiet moments in Paris.

This British tour was the end of a farewell world tour, during which he had visited Australasia, Japan and the Middle East, as well as most of Europe. He said that touring was exhausting, and yet it was necessary for promoting one's music. He expressed pleasure at the thought of getting away from the constant glare of publicity, as he had realised that he wanted to spend some time on his own.

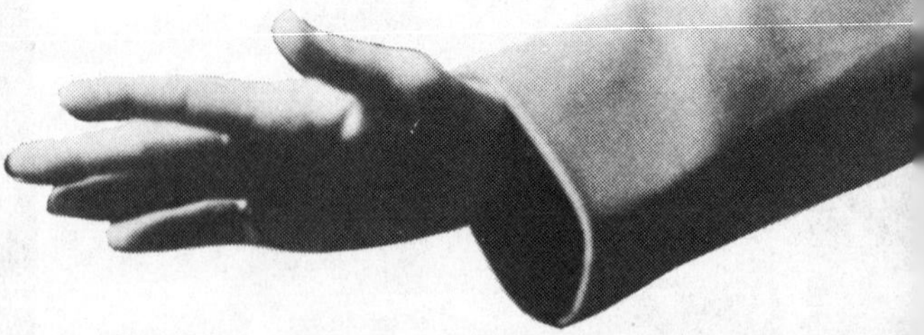

David stated, 'I've been travelling now for three months on this tour, and the conditions simply don't exist for establishing a real relationship or for meeting anyone who might become special'. After that tour he left the music scene, merely two years from the time when he had first entered the British Top 20 with *Could It Be Forever*.

He could be back soon. At the moment, during this time of uncertainty, his fans are doubtless playing *How Can I Be Sure, Cherish, I'll Meet You Halfway*, and all the other discs he recorded between 1972 and 1974!

sidy

RCA News
RCA Limited | Record Division

Release February 21, 1975

DAVID CASSIDY SIGNS EXCLUSIVE, LONG-TERM CONTRACT WITH RCA RECORDS

RCA RECORDS has signed David Cassidy to an exclusive long-term recording contract, it was announced in New York this week by Kenneth Glancy, President of the company.

In welcoming the artist to RCA, Glancy said, "David Cassidy already has made a major contribution to the world of entertainment. But we at RCA feel confident that his future as a performer, composer, and lyricist, will far surpass his previous accomplishments. We are proud to be associated with a proven artist of his stature, and look forward to presenting his talent to its widest possible audience.

"RCA recognizes the potential of a multi-talented individual like David Cassidy, who has weathered a unique type of superstardom very early in his career, with the result that his concentration can now be directed towards becoming an artist of very <u>lasting</u> significance.

"We feel that the long-term, exclusive contract between RCA and David Cassidy, which was negotiated by his manager, Ruth Aarons, expresses a spirit of commitment -- to David's future, and to the future of the label. We look forward to a long and lasting relationship."

-oOo-

Well of course Soul music has been around for many years but take a look at the record charts and what do they all say? Soul is big!

It's all suddenly happened again in the last few years and for most people the North of England has given the rest of Britain the lead. There the disco scene is the most incredible thing, with regular sessions lasting 12 hours or more and often right through to the early hours of morning.

In the North, too, rare Soul records have fetched the most amazing prices—often £30 and sometimes more for one Soul single. Such was the case, for instance, with *Landslide* by an American singer called Tony Clarke.

When the record company realised this they soon re-released the record and the same story has happened for other discs. Many record organizations send their possible release discs to DJs and then ask them how people react to the record. If the response is positive, the record companies release the discs on to the general record market.

There is considerable variation in Soul. Some people would say there is 'sweet' Soul, and this has usually stemmed from the American city of Philadelphia. It is also more often than not the production work of a very talented gentleman called Thom Bell, with words by Humble and Guff. Among 'sweet' Soul groups are The Stylistics, New York City, Detroit Emeralds and The Tymes.

Other people would say that Soul should have more 'funk'—a more pronounced beat—and be just right for dancing. Here some would name groups and artists

Joseph Stevens

such as Graham Central Station, Earth, Wind and Fire, Bloodstone and James Brown.

Then there is a 'romantic' Soul feel from people such as Barry White, Love Unlimited and Minnie Ripperton. Certainly the list of names and talent is endless. There are some amazing sounds in the Soul bracket to be heard from The Ohio Players, Aretha Franklin, B.T. Express and The Tavares. If Soul has usually been found only with black singers and groups, then there is also today a number of white bands putting real funk into their music. Two of these are The Average White Band and Kokomo.

Reggae has been with us for many years and at certain times people have believed that this music will reign supreme. Every now and then the record charts in Britain have reggae

Joseph Stevens

hits in their listings, but an outbreak of reggae almost took Great Britain by storm in 1974 and 1975 when Ken Boothe, John Holt, Susan Cadogan and Tito Simon arrived. Ken, Susan and John made the Top 10, and reggae record fans felt that their dream was fulfilled.

The dream was not realised, however, but look back over the past few years and note the reggae sounds in the charts. There was *Young, Gifted and Black* from Bob and Marcia. In 1969 Desmond Dekker had no less than three Top 20 hits—*007*, *The Israelites* and *It Mek.* And remember Dave and Ansell Collins with *Double Barrel* and *Monkey Spanner?* And how about the group called Greyhound? They had a hit in 1971 called *Black and White,* followed by another hit *Moon River* in 1972. There was also *Let Your Yeah Be Yeah* from The Pioneers and Nicky Thomas made the Top 20 with *Love Of The Common People.*

Two people in particular have always shone. Their names are Jimmy Cliff and Johnny Nash. Jimmy has had hits with *Wild World*—a song written by Cat Stevens—and the catchy song *Wonderful World, Beautiful People.* Johnny has introduced his own distinctive brand of reggae with records such as *Stir It Up, I Can See Clearly Now, There Are More Questions Than Answers, Cupid, You Got Soul* and *Hold Me Tight.* He's also made some very good albums.

So there have been several reggae hits in the charts throughout the past few years. What has been interesting to note is the number of white artists, such as Elton John, The Rolling Stones and Paul Simon, who have travelled to the recording studios in Jamaica to try to capture the reggae sound on their records. Eric Clapton's album *There's One In Every Crowd* managed to do this very well.

For anyone wanting a basic grounding in reggae there are plenty of very good, cheaply-priced compilation sets such as those from Trojan Records called *Tighten Up*—most of the artists and songs on these sets are favourites with the West Indian community.

Often as many as 100 singles are released each week in Britain, though only a few ever make the charts. The chart failure rate is shown by figures which have been issued for 1973 and 1974. Out of 4,327 singles issued in 1973 there were only 253 new chart entries. In 1974 there were 298 chart entries out of 4,034 record releases. To put it another way—in 1973, 3,974 records failed to make the Top 50 and 3,736 failed in 1974!

When *Record Mirror* readers were asked to name their favourite Cliff songs they chose 1 *The Young Ones* 2 *The Day I Met Marie* 3 *Livin' Doll* 4 *Summer Holiday* and 5 *Bachelor Boy*. This result was published near the end of 1973, but it would be interesting to know what people would choose now. What would be your choice?

Before Steeleye Span became known as such, other names for the group were suggested. Tim, backed by Maddy, suggested their name from the song *Horkstow Grange*. Two other early members, Terry and Gay Woods, who have since left, preferred 'Iyubidan Waits' (a 'wait' is an old English band). Tyger Hutchings suggested 'Middlemarch Wait', for Tyger was then very much an admirer of Thomas Hardy. However, as we know, Tim and Maddy won, and for the *Gaudete* hit group it sounds the best name.

Clifford T. Ward is very concerned about spastic children and has given several concerts to raise money for them. His daughter Debbie is a spastic and on his album *Mantle Pieces* Clifford has recorded a lovely song called *To Debbie And Her Friends*.

By 1980 EMI's tape and record sales are expected to reach at least £3,000 million! Their sales figures for 1974 indicate sales of records and tapes worth about £1,000 million.

With only a few exceptions, the album *Bridge Over Troubled Water* by Simon and Garfunkel has been in the record charts for over three years.

Over 56 countries bought or broadcast the BBC Radio One series *The Story of Pop*. The 26-part series was introduced by Alan Freeman, while Tim Blackmore and Keith Skues were two of the many people who were involved in the compilation and production of the series.

There are over 170 record companies in Britain and, although many of these do not produce records which enter any charts, they are able to keep in business because of their sales of specialist records and budget albums which sell for less than £1.

An amazing record was achieved by Elton John with his album *Captain Fantastic And The Brown Dirt Cowboy*. Elton's album went straight to the Number One position in all of the three major American charts. No artist has ever before achieved this in the history of American pop music.

The price of a single at 55p is derived from the following costs—VAT takes 4.1p, copyright takes 3.2p, the artist's royalty is usually 5.6p, the shop takes 20.7p, and recording costs, manufacturing, distribution and marketing take 21.4p.

Even the mighty world of pop can make mistakes! One of the major errors which occurred in 1975 was when 1,000 copies of The Stones' single *I Don't Know Why* were released. In this particular case the wrong composer and music publisher were credited on the record—the song was co-written by Stevie Wonder and not by Mick Jagger, Keith Richard and Mick Taylor as the record stated.

Two's company! Here's something you can do together with a friend. Have fun filling in the word bubbles coming out of your stars' mouths! What could Rod Stewart be saying to Paul and Linda McCartney, who unexpectedly joined him on stage during The Faces' British tour in 1975? And what comments could Les Grey be making as he prepares to go on stage to perform with Dave, Rob and Dave, the other members of Mud? See who can think of the best remarks—it all depends on you!

ay!

CROSSWORDS

(*Clues sometimes when apposite refer to christian or surnames*)

Across

1 Beeb's opener
5 No to a girl was their song in 1971
7 Sunny seasons
8 Sent from above was their song in 1971
9 First word of Slade song
10 Irish and beautiful
11 The seven is missing
12 Once a Scottish bass player with Rollers connections
13 Cockney born (surname)
16 (3) Part of a Welsh duo. See next clue
18 (3) Put humour in charts
21 A lady with a hit from Oxford
23 Initials of Verity's father
24 White, oh white was the face
25 Went travelling with a circus tent

Down

2 Part-time farmer in Scotland
3 Graham or Johnny
4 Football fan
6 No song about winter, only summer
12 Johnny R
13 First word of a Dawn song
14 Lighthouse
15 They began with Na Na
17 The - - - - Of You minus four letters
19 Mac - - - Katie
20 Loves wearing suits
22 Opposite to p.m. radio time

Across

1 (5) Wolverhampton film stars
2 (2) Work it out from 3 across
3 (5) To be watched
6 From Edinburgh
7 Of the world
9 Of decision
10 Musical instrument
12 Over 60 LPs in US charts
14 First part of group name
15 Half of album
18 And over
20 Started own label in 1975
22 Once with Barry
23 A king

Down

1 He says keep a grip on love
2 Spoken hit
4 Third word of Peter's song
5 B.T.
7 If turned round, first word before 'and my dog'
8 His song title goes on bread
10 Same christian name as a Prime Minister
11 People play them, here just one with love
13 Said twice by the clown
16 Reggae
17 An 'L' missing
19 Gypsy
20 Happened that a band were on the . . .
21 Swedish and minus a 'B'

CROSSWORDS

Across

1 (2) 3 (3) 5 (3) Part of song title
8 Not fm
9 Carshalton
10 Fun on *If*—half the duo
11 Dance
13 Sea-side shuffling
14 Paul's ex-singing partner
15 A house of one who built living accommodation
17 Not just for one
19 Radio station in US and a hit song
21 (6) and (4) how long, he sang
22 Walking boots
26 First and third letters of US hit group
27 Two of the group met on a rugby field (half of name)

Down

2 Without apostrophe, opening word for a Cilla song
4 A disc just out is a . . .
6 By day
7 On Virgin Records (7) and (5)
11 Pop paper
12 From Nottinghamshire and the 'E' is missing here plus other half of name
16 Take a Teddy Bear around
17 Tip- . . . amongst the tulips
18 Stardust
19 Geoff's group once
20 All 78s were this way
21 Sweet and foxy and on the - - -
23 First two letters of horse group
24 Ward
25 Spencer Davis has one

Across

1 Liquid or plastic
5 Once with Brian
6 From Bell to RCA goes this person. Initials only
7 (and 8 down) Run their own affairs
9 Half a duo
11 Wembley recording studios in early times they did play
12 Brum-based
14 Christian name of someone who helps Elton
16 Friend of Dave Mount
17 When letters reversed a Vertigo group. Initials only
19 American singer (Christian name)
20 Put it before jerker
22 A hit of June, 1970
23 Electrician
24 Tamla label hit
26 Once with Elton years ago
27 Half a music hit

Down

1 Christian name of new chart lady in 1975
2 Initials of group
3 Patti's sister
4 Of banjo fame and Scottish birth
5 A third and fifth letter of Freda's name
6 From Bradford (surname only)
7 (5) and (4) Arrested by mistake
8 Goes with 7 across
10 Defence
13 Taught for a time
15 To do with the Chi-Lites and part of a song hit
18 Most groups and singers do them
20 Number one
21 Friends with David
24 Short way for writing Roy Wood's record company
25 They choose release material, no need for the 'and'

FA
CL

All prices are

The Osmonds, Slade and David Essex are just three stars with very good fan clubs. Of course there are umpteen others, because recently fan clubs have become very important again. A few years ago, artists and their managers appeared to have become bored with the fan club idea, but they found their lack of interest challenged by the people who wanted to know more about the stars—the fans.

Simply because a fan club is formed, however, doesn't mean that the club will necessarily be any good. Also, if the organisers do have very good ideas, they can be totally overwhelmed by letters and requests. At the worst, you can wait for a very long time for your membership, and when it does arrive, all you receive is a few scraps of paper containing information about your star, a tin badge, maybe a photo, and a heap of envelopes addressed either to the club, or to you for your reply from them.

However, there are some very good clubs around. Possibly the biggest is The Osmonds' fan club, the membership numbers of which are now over 112,000! The lady in charge is a friendly person called Maureen Street, and the club address is The Osmonds Fan Club, c/o Maureen Street, London, W1A 4YE. The membership fee is 85p. The club changes the content of information every year, and grade the members according to years of membership. A new member receives a 'first year' member's kit which incorporates an impressive range of interesting material, wrapped in cellophane, on The Osmonds. The contents of the first year kit also include an Osmonds' secret

Kate Simon

N
BS

subject to change

Kate Simon

code, badge, vouchers, poster, flexi-disc, biographies and special wallet information.

The David Essex fan club's address is P.O. Box 37, Waltham Cross, Herts, EN8 7EF, and membership costs 90p. Every new member is sent a fan club folder, and an interesting letter written by David. Members receive a xerox copy of this letter but every two months, one member receives the actual letter written by David! There is also a photo of David, some information about his life history by his manager, and a message from David on a flexi-disc.

Slade run their fan club by means of a computer! The entry fee is 80p, and the address is Slade Fan Club, P.O. Box 4SF, London, W1A 4SF. Members receive six newsletters a year, Slade discography and information on Slade merchandise.

One of the newest clubs is for Kenny, the group of *The Bump* and *Fancy Pants* fame. They operate from Ros, 74a Kensington Park Road, London, W.11.

Some other addresses are: **Gary Glitter,** c/o Sue Drake, P.O. Box 78, London, E18 2HW. **Hello,** P.O Box 1BT, London, W1A 1BT. **The Rubettes,** P.O. Box 39, Stockport, Cheshire, SK3 8SU. **Queen,** c/o Pat and Sue, Trident Productions, 3 St Anne's Court, London, W.1 (costing 75p). **The Bay City Rollers,** 27 Preston Grange Road, Prestonpans, East Lothian, Scotland (costing 50p). **David Bowie,** London, W1A 4ND. **Barry Blue,** c/o Carole, 83 George Street, London, W.1.

Remember that you may have to wait a few weeks or even a month or so before you receive your membership information after applying to a fan club.

STAR SIGNS

Capricorn (*22 December-19 January*)
Capricorn subjects know depression and are often miserable for hours or even days at a stretch, because their ruling planet is Saturn. They are very serious people and rarely enjoy light conversation. On the other hand, they are very ambitious and determined. Their favourite colours are usually black, brown and dark green, and interestingly enough, Capricornians are listed as possible musicians!
December: Noel Edmonds (22); Ariel Bender (23); Kenny Everett (25); Phil Spector (26); Ray Thomas (29); *January*: Morgan Fisher (1); David Bowie (8); Elvis Presley (8); Rod Stewart (10); Phil Manzanera (11); Bob Bradbury (14); Peter Oliver (14).

Aquarius (*20 January-18 February*)
Aquarius-born people often daydream and have plenty of ideas, but they are difficult to get to know really well. They frequently have a rebellious streak in their nature, and can be rather tactless. Electric blue is their colour, and they are often writers or scientists.
January: Eric Stewart (20); Tony Blackburn (29); Steve Marriott (29); *February*: Melanie (3); Alex Harvey (5); Mike Batt (6); Alan Lancaster (7); Mick Robertson (14); Lyn Paul (16).

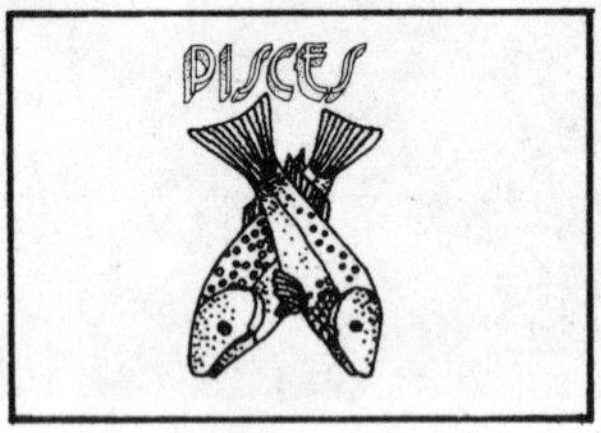

Pisces (*19 February-20 March*)
Pisceans can be compassionate and kind, although they also tend to be careless and indecisive at times. They can also be cheated, if they're not careful, by people who take advantage of their easy-going nature. The arts, such as acting, dancing and writing, feature strongly in the kind of career they might follow.
February: Steve Priest (23); George Harrison (25); Stuart Wood (25); Johnny Cash (26); Vic Faulkner (27); *March:* Roger Daltrey (1); Jay Osmond (2); Dave Mount (3); Jeff Alan (8); James Taylor (12); Neil Sedaka (13); Derek Longmuir (19).

Aries (*21 March-19 April*)
People born under the sign of Aries are capable of very courageous actions and are somewhat adventurous. They can be rather blunt in what they say, and often have quick tempers and selfish natures. They can be impatient and bossy, and like to take the lead in anything they do.
March: Elton John (25); Diana Ross (26); Terry Jacks (29); Graeme Edge (30); *April*: Ronnie Lane (1); Dave Hill (4); Les Grey (9); Phil Wright (9); David Cassidy (12); Al Green (13); Dave Edmunds (15); Jimmy Osmond (16); Eve Graham (19).

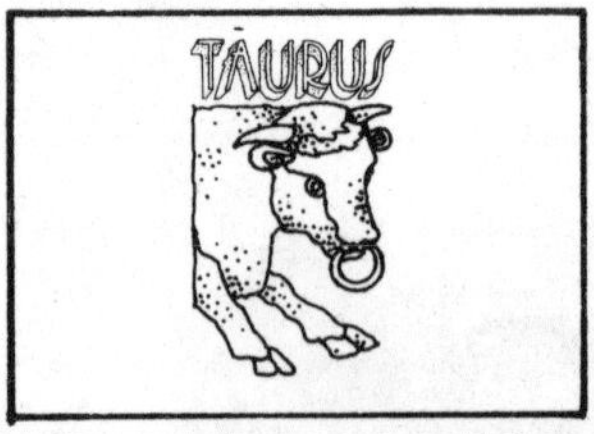

Taurus (*20 April-21 May*)
Taureans can be trusted, as they are very practical and have a strong sense of morals. They are also affectionate, but they make no pretence about those people whom they dislike. They can also be lazy and self-centred.
April: Ed Stewart (23); John Christie (26); Eddie Jobson (28); Merrill Osmond (30); *May:* Jimmy Ruffin (7); Gary Glitter (8) Richard Hudson (9); Graham Gouldman (10); Donovan (10); Ian McLagan (12); Stevie Wonder (13); Paul Thompson (13); Overend Watts (13); Pete Townshend (19).

STAR SIGNS

Gemini (*22 May-20 June*)
Gemini people can apply themselves to many things and are talkative, witty and lively, with an inability to concentrate on any one thing for too long. They often become journalists, broadcasters, lecturers, telephone operators and shop assistants. There's nothing like variety!
May: Bernie Taupin (22); Bob Dylan (24); Marty Kristian (27); Cilla Black (27); Francis Rossi (29); Danny Finn (30); Junior Campbell (31); *June:* Suzi Quatro (3); Ian Hunter (3); Keef Marshall (5); Ron Wood (6); Jon Lord (9); Lynsey de Paul (11), Jim Lea (14); Rod Argent (14); Noddy Holder (15); James Brown (17); Paul McCartney (18); Rick Price (19); Alan Longmuir (20).

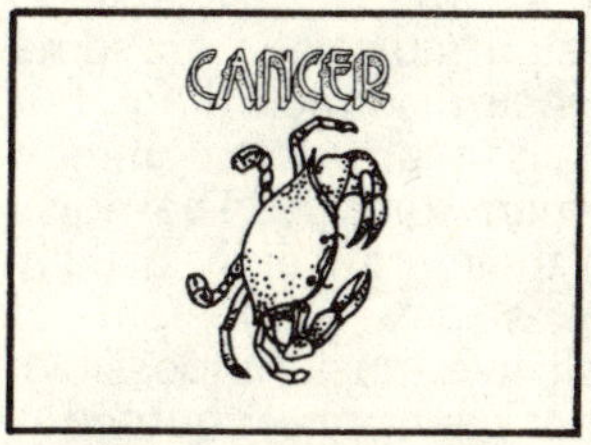

Cancer (*21 June-22 July*)
Bad aspects of Cancer subjects are temper, over-reaction, untidiness and the tendency to keep things to themselves. On the good side they are kind, imaginative and have lots of common sense!
June: Alan Osmond (22); Colin Blunstone (24); Jeff Beck (24); Andy Scott (30); *July:* John Ford (1); Alan Freeman (6); Ringo Starr (7); Andy Fraser (7); Mick Tucker (7); John Ford (18); Brian May (19); Cat Stevens (21).

Leo (*23 July-22 August*)
Leo people have a very generous streak and they are usually quite creative. On the negative side, they can tend to fall in love with themselves and can be rather scornful. They like to be admired and praised.
July: Andy MacKay (23); David Essex (23); Mick Jagger (26); Roger Taylor (26); Mick Vaughan (27); Peter Doyle (28); Simon Kirke (28); *August:* Cliff Fish (13); Paul Layton (14); Johnny Nash (19); John Deacon (19); Phil Lynott (20).

Virgo (*23 August-22 September*)
Virgoans tend to be very fussy and neat, and they have a due sense of modesty. They set high ideals for everybody else around them and tend to criticize everything—so they often tend to miss out on a lot of the good things in life.
August: Keith Moon (23); Rick Springfield (23); Wayne Osmond (28); Michael Jackson (29); Van Morrison (31); *September:* Don Powell (10); Paul Kossoff (14); Kenny Jones (16); John Coghlan (19); Lol Creme (19).

Libra (*23 September-22 October*)
Those people born under the sign of Libra usually have easy-going natures and a lot of charm. However, they do tend to be indecisive and to swing from one emotion to another very quickly. They can also be very stubborn.
September: Linda McCartney (24); Freddie Mercury (25); Stuart Tosh (26); Brian Ferry (26); Olivia Newton-John (26); Marc Bolan (30); *October*: Rob Davis (1); Brian Connolly (5); Kevin Godley (7); John Lennon (9); Marie Osmond (13); Cliff Richard (14); Eric Faulkner (21).

Scorpio (*23 October-21 November*)
Scorpio people have very determined natures and a strong sense of purpose. They can be jealous and resentful, and they do not like to be thwarted. They often prefer to be on their own, and tend to be extreme in their emotions—either loving or hating with great intensity.
October: Dale Griffin (24); Bill Wyman (24); David Paton (29); Jimmy Savile (31); *November:* Chris Morris (1); Joni Mitchell (7); Roy Wood (8); Les McKeown (12); Ray Stiles (20); Simon Turner (21).

Sagittarius (*22 November-21 December*)
Sagittarians tend to make a habit of saying the wrong things at the wrong time! This is because of their frankness and open-mindedness. They are somewhat unconventional and unsentimental, and can sometimes be rather irresponsible. However, they love their freedom and they like to be individualistic.
November: John Rossall (26); *December:* Gilbert O'Sullivan (1); Barry Blue (4); Jonathan King (6); Donny Osmond (9); Jermaine Jackson (11); Rosko (12); Paul Rodgers (17); Keith Richard (18).

POP THE QUE

Am I right in thinking more and more records are warped?
The record companies always deny this, but most record shop owners would tend to agree with you. Many of these warped discs will play on high-quality stereo equipment, but not on equipment costing less than £100. In any case, you should not expect to buy a warped record, whatever the cost of your equipment.

How much should I pay for good stereo equipment?
This is a hard question to answer, but in very broad terms you will have to pay over £100 for a reasonable set-up. Basically, you need two speakers, an amplifier, and a deck with a turntable. You can add a tuner, tape-deck and cheaper accessories such as headphones at a later date. How much you pay depends on where you propose to use the equipment, since there is little point in having powerful equipment if you can never use it to its full potential—if, for example, you live in a small house.

It's useful to consult *Which?* magazine on hi-fi equipment, and a publication such as *Hi-Fi In The Home* by John Crabbe which is published by Blandford. Ensure that there is some form of follow-up, such as a guarantee for repairs, in case anything should go wrong with your equipment. Hi-fi equipment carries a considerable mark-up on prices so check them carefully, as they can differ drastically from one shop to another.

Why do so many groups spend a great deal of time playing to American audiences and not to British ones?
The answer lies in money. In America a group can play to audiences of 10,000 to 20,000, and do so many times on a tour. In Britain it is difficult to find a hall of a suitable size, and those venues which do hold many thousands of people are usually not available for one reason or another.

America also has more cities with larger populations than Britain has, and therefore there are potentially more people in America to populate audiences. For example, some American universities have about 15,000 students.

Why have pop magazines decreased in number and why are those that still exist so expensive?
Paper and ink costs have rocketed over the past few years, and wages of magazine staff have also risen to some extent. These price increases are reflected in the higher costs of magazines. Advertising, the mainstay of all magazines, also tends to decrease during times of economic depression, which means that either the magazines are forced to put their prices up even higher in order to make up for the loss of revenue, or else they go out of business and cease to be published.

Where can I get tour programmes from?
Assuming the company still operates at the time of printing, the address to write to is Theatregraphics, 13 Oxford Circus Avenue, 213 Oxford Street, London, W.1

Is it true that The Bay City Rollers do not play their own instruments on records?
Who really knows? Certainly they have used session musicians on some of their disc recordings but this is a practice common to many groups. The noise at their concerts usually makes any judgement of their live music impossible. What cannot be doubted is the affection the group receive, their massive record sales and their ability to draw audiences.

Can you tell me which were the first television pop programmes?
The first was *6.5 Special*. This began on 16 February 1957 and doubtless your parents used to watch it. It was introduced by Jose-

STION

phine Douglas and Pete Murray, and was broadcast on BBC, whereas the next two shows which followed were made by ABC Television. These were *Oh Boy!* and *Boy Meets Girl.* Both began in 1959 but the former was easily the most popular. *Oh Boy!* was screened for two years, but the same year saw the introduction of a new BBC programme which was to last for a very long time. This was called *Juke Box Jury* and was introduced by David Jacobs. Other programmes preceding *Top Of The Pops*, which began in 1964, were *Wham* (ABC), *Thank Your Lucky Stars* (ABC) which was compèred by Brian Matthew, and *Ready Steady Go* (Rediffusion). *Ready Steady Go,* which ran from 1963 to 1967, had life and spontaneity which has never really been captured since by any other programme. It was also the first television pop programme to be broadcast live, since artists had mimed to their records on previous programmes.

Top Of The Pops is the longest-running television pop show, and it shows no signs of being deleted from BBC schedules in the foreseeable future.

Recently a number of independent television companies have begun their own pop programmes, and some of these have received virtual national networking, as in the case of *45*.

My parents often talk about the Twist. What was it?

The King of Twist was Chubby Checker — real name Ernest Evans—who made his first hit in 1961 with *The Pony.* His next hit was in 1962 and was called *The Twist,* which was followed by *Let's Twist Again*. The dance which followed the discs was denounced by spine specialists as liable to cause physical deformity. It involved considerable gyration and some people swore that it was a positive means of reducing the waistline! In its time the Twist was one of the most popular dances.

Can you tell me how many people buy certain kinds of records?

There are no statistics to indicate this, although EMI, the largest record company, does supply information in percentage terms. They say that 49 per cent of all their record sales are for pop; 30 per cent for middle of the road or easy listening; 10 per cent for classical records; seven per cent for compilation albums; two per cent for jazz music; and one per cent each for children's records and spoken word discs.

What exactly are platinum, gold and silver discs?

A platinum disc is awarded to an artist or group for sales of their record amounting to £1,000,000. A gold disc is awarded for sales of a record reaching £250,000, though prior to September 1974 a gold disc was given for sales of a record amounting to £150,000. A silver disc is awarded for sales reaching £75,000.

Can you tell me more about Pan's People?

Pan's People spend hours and hours perfecting their dance routines for their weekly appearance on *Top Of The Pops.* They run all parts of their career too—fan mail, contracts, costumes, gig times, travelling and publicity.

In case you have designs on becoming a member of Pan's People then you should know that your dance training must already be well advanced. Flick states that 'Seventeen years of age is too late. By the time one is 13 or 14 the muscles have already begun to set, so the earlier you start to train the better. From an early age one must practice and exercise for one hour a day at the very least. Therefore most of our potential dancers come from dancing schools.'

CARPENTERS

A. & M. Records Ltd.

They've taken almost all the world by storm with their immaculately recorded discs, and even some heavy rock fans have expressed their approval of this singing family duo. They've accumulated gold records which reach into double figures and they have also received many Grammy awards.

Richard remembers being involved with records even before he could walk, as their house was always filled with music. At the age of 12 he was playing the piano and by the age of 16 he was studying the classical piano at Yale University, and lying about his age so that he could play the piano in local jazz clubs. And Karen ? By the age of 16 she was one of the youngest-ever female drummers.

In 1965 The Carpenter Trio was launched, with Richard playing the piano, Karen playing the drums, and a friend, Wes Jacobs, playing the tuba and bass. They entered the Hollywood Bowl Battle of the Bands in Los Angeles, and won a number of trophies.

Later, the trio expanded into a band called Spectrum, but hard times came, as their soft rock sound wasn't successful at that time, so the group disbanded. However, Richard and Karen continued with their struggle to become stars, and took samples of their music to countless producers and managers. The two blended their voices into four, six and eight part harmonies and when the producer, Jack Daugherty, heard their sound, he immediately signed up the duo with a record contract !

They made their first album *Offering*, and recorded the Beatle song *Ticket To Ride* as a single, which was very successful. Their second album *Close To You* was also an enormous hit and in 1970 their song *For All We Know* won an Oscar for the 'Best Song Of The Year From A Motion Picture', the title of the film concerned being *Lovers And Other Strangers.* During the same year they also won a Grammy award for being the 'Best New Group' and 'Best Vocal Duo', and they completed amazingly successful tours of umpteen countries.

Those successes were years ago, but their hits have continued. In Britain, they have appeared in the singles charts with such records as *Close To You*, *Superstar, Goodbye To Love, Yesterday Once More, Top Of The World, Please Mister Postman, Jambalaya* and *I Won't Last Another Day Without You.* Their hit albums include *The Carpenters 1969-73, Carpenters, Close To You, Ticket To Ride*, and *Now And Then.*

Richard has remarked of the duo, 'We come along as average people and, because we're not painting our faces, and because we dress up for a performance, we're not hip'. And of their fans, he has stated that he pays close attention to what their public seems to like and the duo respect their wishes. Both Karen and Richard claim that music will always remain a part of their lives—much to their thousands of fans' relief !

QUICK QUIZZES

Just how well do you know the facts? Here is your chance to find out! Remember, no looking at the answers on page 80.

Name the star or group who had a hit with these songs:
1 *I Hear You Knocking*. 2 *Band Of Gold*. 3 *Mary Had A Little Lamb*. 4 *Tap Turns On The Water*. 5 *Hallelujah Freedom*. 6 *School's Out*. 7 *The First Time I Ever Saw Your Face*. 8 *Amanda*. 9 *Give Me Love*. 10 *Summer (The First Time)*.

With which artists or groups do you associate the following songs:
1 *Wanderin' Star*. 2 *Helen Wheels*. 3 *Tweedle Dee Tweedle Dum*. 4 *Questions*. 5 *Getting A Drag*. 6 *I've Been Hurt*. 7 *Witches Promise/Teacher*. 8 *Ernie (The Fastest Milkman In The West)*. 9 *Ben*. 10 *I Believe In Love*.

Guess the song title from the clue: An example to set you going. Clue: All the pack. Answer: *Deck of Cards*.
1 Belongs to the circus. 2 About a gun. 3 Covers the tear. 4 Blows things up. 5 Sometimes when it rains. 6 In tea or coffee. 7 Out of doors. 8 Ever so careful. 9 When nations fight. 10 When you're tired.

Guess the artist or group from the clue: An example to help. Clue: Every day. Answer: Dawn.
1 Top of your list. 2 On toast. 3 Bad car drivers drive there. 4 When they get loose. 5 Jesus lived there. 6 On the American East Coast. 7 A chicken in an H Bomb. 8 Birds have them. 9 On the farm. 10 Replaces grass on football pitches.

Decide the song title from the clue: An example of this. Clue: Up a tree. Answer: *Apeman*.
1 A bear. 2 Not stirring at all. 3 First of the year. 4 Not boys. 5 When you've let it drop. 6 Begging the man who comes every day but Sundays and public holidays. 7 They go round and round. 8 Artificial flowers. 9 Mirror-gazers. 10 When you're with the right one.

Work out the artists by putting the letters in the right order.
1 Xryo. 2 Liopt. 3 Mssdnoo. 4 Dsael. 5 Xof. 6 Arstplig. 7 Eellalb. 8 Ayrnog. 9 Nonnle. 10 Lleehsy.

Guess the year in which these records were first Top 20 hits:
1 *Coz I Luv You*. 2 *My Coo Ca Choo*. 3 *Part Of The Union*. 4 *Shout*. 5 *Everlasting Love*. 6 *Bye Bye Baby*. 7 *Maggie May*. 8 *Stuck In The Middle With You*. 9 *War*. 10 *Photograph*.

One of the three titles given here was the artist or group's first hit. Choose the right one.
1 *a All Right Now*. *b Wishing Well*. *c My Brother Jake*. 2 *a My Friend Stan*. *b Look Wot You Dun*. *c Get Down And Get With It*. 3 *a Angel*. *b Maggie May*. *c You Wear It Well*. 4 *a Rock Me Baby*. *b Daydreamer*. *c Could It Be Forever*. 5 *a Got To Be There*. *b Ben*. *c Ain't No Sunshine*. 6 *a Daniel*. *b Your Song*. *c Goodbye Yellow Brick Road*. 7 *a ABC*. *b Doctor My Eyes*. *c I Want You Back*. 8 *a Roll Away The Stone*. *b All The Young Dudes*. *c Honaloochie Boogie*. 9 *a Lady Rose*. *b In The Summertime*. *c Baby Jump*. 10 *a Close To You*. *b Yesterday Once More*. *c Superstar*.

Complete these song titles:
1 *Some Kind Of* . . . 2 *Gasoline*... 3 *The Love You* . . . 4 *Please Tell Him* . . . 5 *I'm The Leader* . . . 6 *Killing Me* . . . 7 *Free Electric* . . . 8 *Shame* . . . 9 *Sing A* . . . 10 *The Secrets* . . .

Give their Christian names: (this is an easy one!)
1 Glitter. 2 Skellern. 3 Stevens. 4 Wilson. 5 Withers. 6 Beck. 7 Cash. 8 Christie. 9 Dekker. 10 Reddy.

Which artists or groups recorded these albums:
1 *Every Picture Tells A Story*. 2 *Catch Bull At Four*. 3 *Escalator*. 4 *Streets*. 5 *Tubular Bells*. 6 *On The Level*. 7 *Candles In The Rain*. 8 *Flaming Star*. 9 *Universal Soldier*. 10 *Overnight Success*.

Name the odd one in these lists:
1 *Sleepy Shores*; *Eye Level*; *Mozart Symphony No. 40*; *Candida*.
2 *Storm In A Teacup*; *American Woman*; *Amanda*; *I Say A Little Prayer*.
3 *Bye Bye Baby*; *I Love You Love Me Love*; *Only You Can*; *Lady Marmalade*.
4 *Give Me Love*; *Jet*; *Eleanor Rigby*; *Smarty Pants*.

in lov
MAR

Quite a few young ladi cross their fingers and hop to marry Donny. Maure Street of The Osmonds' fa club says that many of th club's members believe th they have a chance wi

Date of birth: 20 Septemb 19

Star sign: Lib

Place of birth: Hackne East Lond

Height: 5ft 7

Weight: 9st 4

Colour of hair: Dark brov

Colour of eyes: Haz

Favourite colour: Da bl

Favourite musician: Ji Hendr

Favourite group: Ji Hendrix Experien

Favourite book: *Stranger A Strange Land* by Robe Heinlen; and anything abo space ficti

Favourite writer: Robe Heinl

Favourite films: *King Creo* and any other early rock roll fil

Favourite actors: Lau and Har

Favourite actress: No

Favourite food: Cheese a spinach p

Favourite drink: Do Perignon champag

Musical influences: Ji Hend

Other interests: Collecti guitars; the cinem collecting fun posters a pictures, as he believes house should contain a lot objects which are interesti

with
r ROD?

Donny while he is on the oose—whatever the odds! What though of Rod Stewart or Marc Bolan? If you're in ove with either of them, you'd better know these acts first!

Date of birth: 10 January 1944
Star sign: Capricorn
Place of birth: London
Height: 5ft 11in.
Colour of hair: Light brown
Colour of eyes: Hazel
Favourite colours: Bright ones
Favourite musician: Elton John
Favourite group: Elton John
Favourite books: Football books
Favourite writer: Many
Favourite films: Sees a great many, but leaves if bored
Favourite actor: Undecided
Favourite actress: Britt Ekland
Favourite food: Grilled bacon and eggs, ensuring no grease. Dislikes anything fattening
Favourite drink: Bacardi and coke
Musical influences: Rock n' roll; rhythm and blues
Other interests: Mostly football; clothes; collecting things, particularly old silver

Kate Simon

HIT THE CHARTS!

HOW THE WEEKLY TOP 50 IS MADE UP

Tuesday morning is vital to every singer and group in Britain every week of the year, except Bank Holidays, in which case Wednesday becomes the important day. The reason for this is that every Tuesday, the weekly Top 50 chart is announced, in addition to a list which is issued to the music trade of what are known as 'breakers'.

The chart is for singles and to a large degree it dictates shop ordering of records, and encourages radio play. As any artist will tell you, the world follows two charts—the American and the British—and therefore the Top 50 chart leads to record release for artists elsewhere throughout the world. This consequently leads to a greater possibility of public appearances in other countries too.

The successful solo artists and groups whose records are in the Top 50 but who are without disc release in the United States also have a stronger case for Stateside issue if their record is in the British Top 50.

Where the charts are used

The Top 50 is used by the BBC and forms the basis of *Top Of The Pops*, Britain's leading television pop show. Other television networks make use of the chart too, and every week on London Weekend's *Saturday Scene* its compère, Sally James, introduces the Number One record.

The chart is printed in *Record Mirror* and is also published the following week in its sister paper, *Sounds*. It is also to be found in the one trade paper, *Music Week*, and is reprinted across the world by the world's major music paper, *Billboard*.

There are other charts. A different one is used by both *Melody Maker* and *Disc*, and a further one is compiled by *New Musical Express*, which was the first paper ever to run a chart in the early 1950s.

However, the most important chart is the one compiled by the British Market Research Bureau—a highly professional and long-established research organisation.

How they are compiled

Each week 300 shops are selected on the basis of area, size of shop and type of shop. This ensures that they are representative of conventional record outlets. Each shop compiles a diary in which a record is kept of the serial number of each single and album which has been sold that week. Diaries are posted on Saturday after the shops close and are received by the B.M.R.B. on Mondays.

Diaries are checked and any blank spaces are cancelled, to avoid any possible interference by staff. Entries are carefully scrutinized, and if a block of the same catalogue number occurs then the shop concerned is contacted. There may, of course, be a good reason for so many of one particular record being sold, such as the artist or group playing in that town on a previous evening.

How the charts are tested

The record serial numbers are punched onto cards which are then fed into a computer. On Monday nights the computer counts the sales for each serial number. Each 'new entry' and each 'fast riser' (a single which has risen 10 or more places in the chart since the previous week) is subjected to a statistical test. Fifty shops which are not on the panel are chosen at random and asked questions about their sales of these records. If a record fails to pass this test, the Bureau reserves the right to withdraw the disc from the charts.

When the records have been tested the charts are compiled and sent to the music trade paper *Music Week* and to the BBC. From this emerges the British Top 50 of which the Top 30 is announced on the Tuesday midday record show compèred by Johnnie Walker, on the BBC Radio One network.

Around Britain artists and groups doubtless telephone their record companies, anxious to know at what position their record is in the charts. And for somebody in particular, it could be their Number One week!

POP RECORDS...

A GUIDE TO STARTING YOUR OWN POP LIBRARY

All prices are subject to change.

You will need lots of money to compile a really complete library of pop books because there are so many of them! This chapter deals with the general pop scene and not with specialised tastes such as rock 'n' roll, rhythm and blues or record company histories.

The history of pop

For colour and liveliness there can be few better books on this subject than the arrestingly-titled *Awopbopaloobop Alopbamboom* by Nik Cohn which is published by Paladin and costs 50p. This book outlines the author's likes and dislikes of the stars who rose to fame between the 1950s and the late 1960s, so there is nothing about recent teen heroes such as Slade or The Osmonds.

There is also George Melly's informative paperback called *Revolt Into Style*, which is published by Penguin at 40p.

There is also a general book which is not so much a history of pop as a tracing of certain themes which are connected with the pop world. This is *Understanding Pop* by Tony Jasper which costs £1.95 and is published by SCM Press.

The Story of Pop, published by Octopus at £3.95, contains material which was published weekly in *The Story Of Pop* magazine series which ran in conjunction with the Radio One series of the same name. This book contains many colour pictures in addition to the usual black and white ones.

Two very good paperbacks, *Rock File 1* and *Rock File 2*, are essential for anyone who enjoys following record charts and how the artists have fared over the years. These books are edited by Charlie Gillet, and are published by Panther at 50p.

Lyric books

Early pop songs and late 1960s psychedelic material can be found in *The Poetry Of Rock* by Richard Goldstein, and this is published by Bantam at 40p.

The Beatles' lyrics appear in two glossy and visually appealing volumes called *The Beatle Lyrics* which is published by Macdonald for £1.50. Less expensive and without artwork is *The Beatle Lyrics* which is published by Futura at 40p.

There is also *Today's Sound* and *Sound Seventies* by Tony Jasper which are published by Galliard at 45p and 49p respectively.

Individual stars

George Tremlett has written individual paperbacks on *David Bowie, Gary Glitter, David Essex* and *Marc Bolan* which have been published by Futura costing 40p each.

There is also the *Bay City Rollers'* story which was related by Tam Paton to Michael Wale. This paperback costs 45p and is published by Everest.

There is, of course, Slade's film *Flame*, and there is a paperback of the film published by Panther and written by John Pidgeon which costs 50p.

If you like Bob Dylan, John Lennon, or Ian Hunter, then look out for *Bob Dylan* by Anthony Scaduto (Abacus, 60p); *Lennon Remembers* by John Lennon (Penguin, 40p); and *Diary Of A Rock And Roll Star* by Ian Hunter (Panther, 50p). Joan Baez has also written an autobiography called *Daybreak* which is published by Panther at 35p.

The music business

To enable you to find out about the music business and other subjects relating to it, read *Vox Pop* by Michael Wale which costs £1.50 and is published by Harrap, or *Anatomy Of Pop* by various writers costing 70p which is available from BBC Publications.

Look in your local library for the hardback books mentioned here, and look for the paperbacks in your local bookshops. If you cannot obtain them, then write to the publishers concerned as most of them have sales departments which will be only too pleased to help.

A HUNDRED HITS

	Title	Artist	Label	Year
1	*She Loves You*	**Beatles**	*Parlophone*	(1963)
2	*I Want to Hold Your Hand*	**Beatles**	*Parlophone*	(1963)
3	*Tears*	**Ken Dodd**	*Columbia*	(1965)
4	*Can't Buy Me Love*	**Beatles**	*Parlophone*	(1964)
5	*I Feel Fine*	**Beatles**	*Parlophone*	(1964)
6	*We Can Work It Out*	**Beatles**	*Parlophone*	(1965)
7	*Release Me*	**Engelbert Humperdinck**	*Decca*	(1967)
8	*Green Grass Of Home*	**Tom Jones**	*Decca*	(1966)
9	*Last Waltz*	**Engelbert Humperdinck**	*Decca*	(1967)
10	*The Carnival Is Over*	**Seekers**	*Columbia*	(1965)
11	*I Remember You*	**Frank Ifield**	*Columbia*	(1962)
12	*I Love You Love Me Love*	**Gary Glitter**	*Bell*	(1973)
13	*Stranger On The Shore*	**Acker Bilk**	*Columbia*	(1962)
14	*Long Haired Lover From Liverpool*	**Jimmy Osmond**	*MGM*	(1973)
15	*The Young Ones*	**Cliff Richard**	*Columbia*	(1962)
16	*Eye Level*	**Simon Park Orchestra**	*Columbia*	(1974)
17	*I'd Like To Teach The World To Sing*	**New Seekers**	*Polydor*	(1972)
18	*Tie A Yellow Ribbon*	**Dawn**	*Bell*	(1973)
19	*Sugar Sugar*	**Archies**	*RCA*	(1970)
20	*Bachelor Boy*	**Cliff Richard**	*Columbia*	(1962)
21	*Merry Xmas Everybody*	**Slade**	*Polydor*	(1974)
22	*Two Little Boys*	**Rolf Harris**	*Columbia*	(1969)
23	*Glad All Over*	**Dave Clark Five**	*Columbia*	(1964)
24	*Telstar*	**Tornadoes**	*Decca*	(1962)
25	*You Won't Find Another Fool Like Me*	**New Seekers**	*Polydor*	(1974)
26	*Needles and Pins*	**Searchers**	*Pye*	(1964)
27	*Help*	**Beatles**	*Parlophone*	(1965)
28	*Anyone Who Had A Heart*	**Cilla Black**	*Parlophone*	(1964)
29	*Lovesick Blues*	**Frank Ifield**	*Columbia*	(1962)
30	*Welcome Home*	**Peters and Lee**	*Philips*	(1973)
31	*My Sweet Lord*	**George Harrison**	*Apple*	(1973)
32	*You'll Never Walk Alone*	**Gerry and The Pacemakers**	*Columbia*	(1963)
33	*Claire*	**Gilbert O'Sullivan**	*MAM*	(1973)
34	*Hey Jude*	**Beatles**	*Parlophone*	(1968)
35	*Amazing Grace*	**Royal Scots Dragoon Guards Band**	*RCA*	(1972)
36	*This Will Be The Last Time*	**Rolling Stones**	*Decca*	(1965)
37	*I'll Never Find Another You*	**Seekers**	*Columbia*	(1965)
38	*Are You Sure*	**Allisons**	*Fontana*	(1961)
39	*Blockbuster*	**Sweet**	*RCA*	(1973)
40	*Hard Day's Night*	**Beatles**	*Parlophone*	(1964)
41	*Puppy Love*	**Donny Osmond**	*MGM*	(1973)
42	*My Ding-A-Ling*	**Chuck Berry**	*Mercury*	(1973)
43	*My Coo-Ca Choo*	**Alvin Stardust**	*Magnet*	(1973)
44	*Ernie*	**Benny Hill**	*Columbia*	(1971)
45	*Tiger Feet*	**Mud**	*RAK*	(1974)
46	*From Me To You*	**Beatles**	*Parlophone*	(1963)
47	*I'm A Believer*	**Monkees**	*RCA*	(1967)
48	*Hello Goodbye*	**Beatles**	*Apple*	(1967)

49	*Without You*	**Nilsson**	*RCA*	(1972)
50	*Distant Drums*	**Jim Reeves**	*RCA*	(1966)
51	*Those Were The Days*	**Mary Hopkin**	*Apple*	(1968)
52	*Return To Sender*	**Elvis Presley**	*RCA*	(1962)
53	*Rock-A-Hula Baby*	**Elvis Presley**	*RCA*	(1962)
54	*Grandad*	**Clive Dunn**	*Columbia*	(1971)
55	*Lonely This Christmas*	**Mud**	*RAK*	(1974)
56	*What Do You Want?*	**Adam Faith**	*Parlophone*	(1959)
57	*Lily The Pink*	**Scaffold**	*Parlophone*	(1969)
58	*I Got You Babe*	**Sonny and Cher**	*Atlantic*	(1965)
59	*Pretty Woman*	**Roy Orbison**	*London*	(1964)
60	*Whiter Shade Of Pale*	**Procol Harum**	*Deram*	(1967)
61	*Billy Don't Be A Hero*	**Paper Lace**	*Bus Stop*	(1974)
62	*Gonna Make You A Star*	**David Essex**	*CBS*	(1974)
63	*Bobby's Girl*	**Susan Maughan**	*Philips*	(1962)
64	*Little Children*	**Billy J. Kramer**	*Parlophone*	(1964)
65	*See My Baby Jive*	**Wizzard**	*Harvest*	(1973)
66	*Chirpy Chirpy Cheep Cheep*	**Middle Of The Road**	*RCA*	(1971)
67	*You're My World*	**Cilla Black**	*Parlophone*	(1964)
68	*I Hear You Knocking*	**Dave Edmunds**	*MAM*	(1970)
69	*Wonder Of You*	**Elvis Presley**	*RCA*	(1970)
70	*In The Summertime*	**Mungo Jerry**	*Dawn*	(1970)
71	*Ruby Don't Take Your Love To Town*	**Kenny Rogers and The First Edition**	*Reprise*	(1969)
72	*Crazy Horses*	**Osmonds**	*MGM*	(1973)
73	*Ticket To Ride*	**Beatles**	*Parlophone*	(1965)
74	*Strangers In The Night*	**Frank Sinatra**	*Reprise*	(1966)
75	*My Way*	**Frank Sinatra**	*Reprise*	(1969)
76	*When Will I See You Again*	**Three Degrees**	*Philly*	(1974)
77	*Have I The Right*	**Honeycombs**	*Pye*	(1964)
78	*Seasons In The Sun*	**Terry Jacks**	*Bell*	(1974)
79	*Wonderful World*	**Louis Armstrong**	*HMV*	(1968)
80	*The Show Must Go On*	**Leo Sayer**	*Chrysalis*	(1974)
81	*Cum On Feel The Noize*	**Slade**	*Polydor*	(1973)
82	*The Wedding*	**Julie Rodgers**	*Mercury*	(1964)
83	*Wonderful Land*	**Shadows**	*Columbia*	(1962)
84	*Get Back*	**Beatles**	*Apple*	(1969)
85	*It's Not Unusual*	**Tom Jones**	*Decca*	(1965)
86	*For The Good Times*	**Perry Como**	*RCA*	(1973)
87	*Cinderella Rockafella*	**Esther and Abi Ofarim**	*Fontana*	(1968)
88	*Kung Fu Fighting*	**Carl Douglas**	*Pye*	(1974)
89	*World Without Love*	**Peter and Gordon**	*Columbia*	(1964)
90	*Puppet On A String*	**Sandie Shaw**	*Pye*	(1967)
91	*Paper Roses*	**Marie Osmond**	*MGM*	(1974)
92	*Devil Gate Drive*	**Suzi Quatro**	*RAK*	(1974)
93	*Satisfaction*	**Rolling Stones**	*Decca*	(1965)
94	*She*	**Charles Aznavour**	*Barclay*	(1974)
95	*Sugar Baby Love*	**Rubettes**	*Polydor*	(1974)
96	*Love Me For A Reason*	**Osmonds**	*MGM*	(1974)
97	*Wanderin' Star*	**Lee Marvin**	*Paramount*	(1970)
98	*Dominique*	**Singing Nun**	*Philips*	(1963)
99	*Go Now*	**Moody Blues**	*Decca*	(1965)
100	*All Right Now*	**Free**	*Island*	(1970)

These have been the best-selling singles between 1959 and 1974. Their positions have been derived from the number of sales they have achieved. Reproduced from the Music Week Industry Yearbook by kind permission of Billboard Ltd.

QUEEN ANNE PRESS
Examinations Board
for the Certificate of General Education
1975/1976

POP
PAPERS 1A AND 1B

Complete a, b, and c below in block capitals
a Candidate's name..
b Candidate's address..
....
c Candidate's age..

General notes
1. *Although the sending of the printed paper is preferred, to prevent spoiling the book candidates may copy the complete paper on to normal paper. However, candidates must remember to draw the necessary boxes and to include relevant details such as name and address.*
2. *Candidates achieving a mark of* 80 *or above will receive a special certificate, and candidates passing the examination will receive a special letter stating that they have achieved proficiency in pop.*
3. *Although there will be serious marking of the two papers, it is pointed out that the Certificate of The Queen Anne Press carries no status or merit and cannot be quoted or used in furtherance of any kind of employment or used as a reference of any kind.*
4. *© Tony Jasper. This examination paper is strictly copyright, and must not be used or copied without permission.*
5. *Candidates must enclose a stamped addressed envelope in order to receive a reply containing their examination result. Papers should be sent to* E A *Lower Front Flat,* 67 *Belsize Park Gardens, London, N.W.*3. *Please allow at least one month for a reply.*
6. *No papers can be accepted for marking or award after* 31 *March* 1976.
7. *Candidates are trusted not to use books for reference to the answers!*
8. *The publishers regret that they cannot enter into any form of correspondence regarding the final results of individual papers which will, of course, not be returned.*

PAPER 1A
Time allowed—30 minutes.

For each of the following questions five possible answers are given. Print in the space provided the *code letter* of the answer which you think is correct.
For example, if you think Lady Madonna failed to reach Number One, print b *in the space provided.*

1 Which Beatle title failed to reach Number One in the singles charts?
a From Me To You
b Lady Madonna
c Help
d Please Please Me
e I Feel Fine *Answer:* ....

2 Which Perry Como song reached Number One in the singles charts?
a Kewpie Doll
b Delaware
c And I Love Her So
d It's Impossible
e Magic Moments *Answer:* ....

3 Which Elton John song reached Number Two in the singles charts?
a Daniel
b Crocodile Rock
c Rocket Man
d Philadelphia Freedom
e Your Song *Answer:* ....

4 Which Donny Osmond hit failed to reach a Top Four position?
a Too Young
b Young Love
e Twelfth Of Never
d Why
e Puppy Love *Answer:* ....

In the following questions one record in each list is out of sequence with regard to the year in which the discs were recorded. Print in the space provided the code letter of the answer which you think is correct.
For example, if you think We Will *was recorded before* Nothing Rhymed, *print* b *in the space provided.*

5 a Nothing Rhymed
b We Will
c Alone Again
d No Matter How I Try
e Ooh-Wakka-Doo-Wakka-Day *Answer:* ....

6 a Close To You
b Superstar
c Goodbye To Love
d Top Of The World
e Yesterday Once More *Answer:* ....

7 a Signed, Sealed And Delivered
b Never Had A Dream Come True
c If You Really Love Me
d Superstitition
e You Are The Sunshine Of My Life *Answer:* ....

8 a God Only Knows
b Good Vibrations
c Heroes And Villains
d Then I Kissed Her
e Darlin' *Answer:* ....

9 In the following questions the year in which each record became a hit is required. The code letter for each year is as follows: a—1957, b—1964, c—1965, d—1966, and e—1968.

a Paperback Writer *Answer:* ....

b Move Over Darling *Answer:* ....

c I'm Into Something Good *Answer:* ....

d You Can't Hurry Love *Answer:* ....

e Scarlet Ribbons *Answer:* ....

f Message to Martha *Answer:* ....

g Congratulations *Answer:* ....

10 In the following questions, one artist in each group has been aligned with the wrong record. Print in the space provided the code letter of the answer which you think is correct.
For example, if you believe that Leo Sayer did not record Just a Boy, *print* a *in the space provided.*

a Just A Boy—Leo Sayer
b Autobahn—Kraftwerk
c Stand By Your Man—Tammy Jones
d Take Your Mama For A Ride—Lulu
e Oh Boy—Mud *Answer:* ....

11 a Sha La La—Al Green
b Pepper Box—Peppers
c Tell Him—Hello
d Christmas Song—Slade
e Down Down—Status Quo *Answer:* ....

12 a Little Bitty Tear—Burl Ives
b The Wanderer—Dion
c Lesson Number One—Russ Conway
d I'll Never Find Another You—New Seekers
e Don't Stop, Twist—Frankie Vaughan *Answer:* ....

13 In the answer space, provide the required information. (All hits must have been in the Top 20.)
a Three of Cliff Richard's hits in 1959
i ....
ii ....
iii ....
b Three of Bob Dylan's hits in 1965 or 1966
i ....
ii ....
iii ....
c Three of Neil Sedaka's hits before 1970
i ....
ii ....
iii ....

14 Read the following carefully, and note the four deliberate mistakes in the answer space provided.

'In May of 1973 Stuart Gillies entered the Top 20 with the song *Amanda*. Up to the middle of 1975 this was his only hit. The same year saw The Goons in the charts once more with their 1959 song, *Ying Tong Song*. Albert Hammond had a hit during the same year with *Free Electric Band*. *Give Me Love* from George Harrison was also a 1973 hit and it reached Number Eight in the Top 20. During June of that year Geordie had a hit with *Can You Do It* and this disc reached Number Two, and was their first chart success. *All Because Of You* was their next success, whilst in 1973 Free triumphed with *Wishing Well*.'

a ....
b ....
c ....
d ....

15 Read the following carefully, and note the deliberate mistakes in the answer space provided.

'Cliff Richard has recorded many hit discs on Pye Records, and his first success was *Move It*. The first hit for the Righteous Brothers was *You've Lost That Lovin' Feeling*, and many versions of that song have since been made. *El Paso* was Marty Robbins' first hit and this was in 1960. In 1972 Gary Glitter triumphed with *Rock And Roll Part 2* and he again entered the charts two years later with *Love Like You And Me*. On this disc he was backed by The Glitter Band, who had begun making hits themselves in 1973 when Paul Da Vinci was a member of the group. Gary Glitter was once known as Paul Raven, and he was not Billy Fury.'

 a ....

b ....

c ....

d ....

16 Answer the following questions with a simple yes or no in the answer space provided.

	Yes/No
Aretha recorded *Spanish Harlem*	....
Elvis records for RCA	....
Juliet was a 1965 hit	....
Tears was a 1965 hit	....
The Filmore East is in Philadelphia	....
The Marquee is a famous club in Liverpool	....
The Cavern was in Glasgow	....
Focus recorded *Sylvia*	....
Van Morrison is Irish	....
Two people had a hit in 1957 with *Young Love*	....
Woodstock Festival was in 1968	....
Dana made a hit with *White Horses*	....
Bob Harris is called 'Bomber'	....
Noel Edmonds owns record shops	....

PAPER 1B

Time allowed—60 minutes

Answer the following questions in the spaces provided:

17 Name one distinctive musical style between 1954 and 1956 ....

18 Name the first three records by Pilot ....

....

....

19 Which Number One record stayed at the top of the charts for the longest number of weeks?

....

20 Name the manager of The Bay City Rollers ....

21 Name Elvis Presley's manager..........

22 Who wrote the song *Younger Girls?*..........

23 Who produced *River Deep Mountain High?*..........

24 Where do Bachman Turner Overdrive come from?..........

25 Who is the lead singer of The Rolling Stones?..........

26 Which song by The Who is about a tramp?..........

27 Which group recorded an Eddie Cochran song in 1975?..........

28 Which person connected with Slade once had connections with The Animals? ....

29 Which trio had a hit with *Blowin' In The Wind?* ....

30 Which supergroup included Eric Clapton and Stevie Winwood as members?

....

31 Choose one of the following, write your answer on separate paper, and attach it to your answer sheet:

Either write the lyrics of one pop song which was popular between 1959 and 1969;
or write out the lyrics of one pop song which was popular between 1970 and 1975.
At least three verses and the chorus, if applicable, must be included.

32 In 100-200 words give a brief outline of one of the artists in the following list. Write your answer on paper which is to be enclosed with your answer sheet.

a Joan Baez
b Bay City Rollers
c Bob Dylan
d David Essex
e Elton John
f Led Zeppelin
g Paul McCartney
h Joni Mitchell
i The Moody Blues
j Donny Osmond
k Elvis Presley
l The Rolling Stones
m Slade
n The Supremes
o The Who
p Yes

33 List on separate paper 20 hits from any *one* year from 1959 to the present day. List the artists who recorded the discs as well as the titles.

34 Choose one of the following subjects and list about 20 records (both singles and albums) and the artists who recorded them, which have been connected with the subject you have chosen.

a American West Coast Music (1966 to 1969)
b Rock 'n' Roll (1955 to 1959)
c British and American artists who are in their teens who have been popular in Britain between 1974 and 1975
d Girl singers who have been popular in Britain between 1970 and 1974
e The Philadelphia Sound
f Reggae chart music in Britain from 1968
g British blues music since 1956
h Scottish groups between 1973 and 1975

35 Answer the following questions in the spaces provided:

Name six British record companies

a ....

b ....

c ....

d ....

e ....

f ....

Name six television pop shows since *6.5 Special* (which must not be included).

a ....

b ....

c ....

d ....

e ....

f ....

Name four British or American family duos or groups

a ....

b ....

c ....

d ....

Name five songs which have been hits more than once

a ....

b ....

c ....

d ....

e ....

Name five singers or groups who started recording before 1970, and who have had at least one hit either in the singles or album charts since 1973

a ....

b ....

c ....

d ....

e ....

Check to see that all the answers have been given. Remember to check that all question papers and answer sheets are in the correct order.

This corner must be sent with examination answers, otherwise the paper cannot be marked, and notification of result cannot be obtained.

Pop Exam Entry

ANSWERS

Page 22 1 23 July 1947. **2** Docker. **3** Shipman's Secondary Modern. **4** Sydney Cole's Dance Band. **5** Derek Bowman. **6** West Ham. **7** Rozaa. **8** Paignton Festival Hall. **9** *Dick Whittington.* **10** At a London disco. **11** Jeff Wayne. **12** CBS. **13** No. **14** The Eagle. **15** New Victoria.

Page 24 1 Kan Sai. **2** David Bowie And The Buzz. **3** Three Dog Night. **4** Working in an advertising agency. **5** Terry Cox. **6** *2001—A Space Odyssey.* **7** 18 months. **8** Spiders From Mars. **9** Five. **10** *Aladdin Sane.*

Page 25 1 *Keep Yourself Alone.* **2** *See What A Fool I've Been.* **3** John Anthony, Roy Baker, Queen. **4** Infra-red Astronomy. **5** Biology. **6** Smile. **7** EMI. **8** *Queen II.* **9** 1946. **10** Chris Squires (Yes), Philip Chennla (Butts).

Page 27 1 Faulkner/Wood/McKeown. **2** Pisces. **3** Secondary Modern, Tynecastle. **4** Trainee joiner in an odd job firm. **5** Phil Coulter, Bill Martin. **6** Tweed. **7** Plaice. **8** Bay City, from whence their name comes. **9** 17. **10** Billy and David.

Page 29 1 1950. **2** Blue. **3** Bloxwich, Staffs. **4** Jim Lea. **5** Gemini. **6** Melbourne Arms, Wolverhampton. **7** 5ft 10in. **8** Seven. **9** Stafford Youth Orchestra. **10** Neil Young, Burt Bacharach. **11** Donald George Powell. **12** Police Forces' Boxing Club. **13** Yes. **14** Yes. **15** Charlie. **16** Fleet Castle, Devon. **17** Aries. **18** Grandfather. **19** Brown. **20** Barry. **21** *Wild Winds Are Blowing.* **22** *Coz I Luv You.* **23** Jim Lea. **24** 7 January 1973. **25** Dave Hill.

Page 34 1 1963. **2** 1971. **3** Donald Clark Osmond. **4** Ten. **5** American High School, Heber City, Utah. **6** Her mother. **7** Blue and green. **8** Italy. **9** Pinegor (Suzanne). **10** *Least Of All You.* **11** Blue satin, floor-length gowns. **12** Corky Kooky. **13** Malts. **14** Ogden, Utah. **15** Hamburgers and hot dogs.

Page 35 1 1947. **2** Watford. **3** Reg Dwight. **4** Bernie Taupin. **5** Mid-brown. **6** Yes. **7** Ed Stewart. **8** Guildford. **9** Acting. **10** Ten. **11** 1946. **12** Six. **13** Left. **14** Gordon Mills. **15** 25. **16** London. **17** 5ft. **18** Hornsey College of Art, London. **19** Barry Blue. **20** Five. **21** Law (Business). **22** *The Bump.* **23** Andy Walton. **24** Bill Martin, Phil Coulter. **25** Scotland. **26** Yes. **27** Stuart. **28** *January.* **29** Alvin Stardust. **30** *Love Me Love My Dog.* **31** Marty Wilde. **32** Magnet. **33** Paul McCartney. **34** Liverpool. **35** Scaffold. **36** Yes. **37** John Rossall. **38** Gary Glitter. **39** *Rock 'n' Roll Dudes.* **40** Gerry Shephard. **41** Elizabeth Beresford. **42** Mike Batt. **43** Orinoco. **44** *Minuetto Allegretto.* **45** Wellington.

Page 40 *Kimono My House.* **2** Ron Mael. **3** *Wondergirl.* **4** Halfnelson. **5** Kidderminster. **6** *Home Thoughts.* **7** *Gaye.* **8** Ten. **9** Lowell George. **10** 1971. **11** *Little Feat.* **12** Allen Toussaint. **13** *Crime Of The Century.* **14** Ken Scott. **15** Richard Davies and Roger Hodgson. **16** Dougie Thomson. **17** *Bedsitter Images.* **18** Yes. **19** Alan Parsons. **20** *Orange.* **21** *Listen To The Music.* **22** *Toulouse Street.* **23** *The Captain And Me.* **24** Little John Hartman and Keith Krudsen. **25** David Hamilton.

Page 58 *Across:* **1** Edmonds. **5** Tams. **7** Jacks. **8** Elgins. **9** How. **10** Dana. **11** oo. **12** Paton. **13** Stevens. **16** Yin. **18** Yan. **21** Noosha. **23** DE. **24** Sayer. **25** Lane. *Down:* **2** McCartney. **3** Nash. **4** Stewart. **6** Mungo. **12** Piglets. **13** Say. **14** Edison. **15** Steam. **17** Near. **19** And. **20** Noel. **22** a.m.

Page 58 *Across:* **1** Slade. **2** in. **3** Flame. **6** Eric. **7** End. **9** Year. **10** Moog. **12** Mathis. **14** Led. **15** Sheet. **18** Over. **20** Ringo. **22** Rubettes. **23** Nosmo. *Down:* **1** Skellern. **2** If. **4** Lady. **5** Express. **7** em. **8** Goldsboro. **10** Melvin. **11** Game. **13** Ha. **16** Toots. **17** Ye. **19** Rose. **20** Run. **21** Aba.

Page 59 *Across:* **1** My man and. **8** am. **9** Mud. **10** Yin. **11** Reel. **13** Dactyl. **14** Art. **15** Jack. **17** tea. **19** WOLD. **21** Ronnie Lane. **22** Nancy. **26** OM. **27** Status. *Down:* **2** Youre. **4** Newy. **6** day. **7** Tubular Bells. **11** RM. **12** Lac. **16** Kenny. **17** toe. **18** Adam. **19** Wings. **20** Mono. **21** Run. **23** AM. **24** CT. **25** B.A.

Page 59 *Across:* **1** Minestrone. **5** Eno. **6** DC. **7** Pans. **9** Ike. **11** Queen. **12** ELO. **14** Gus. **16** Ray. **17** LT. **19** Leon. **20** Tear. **22** ABC. **23** Donny. **24** War. **26** Marsha. **27** Eye.
Down: **1** Minnie. **2** NW. **3** Suzi Q. **4** Eric. **5** EA. **6** Dee. **7** Paper Lace. **8** People. **10** Kung. **13** Ferry. **15** Seen. **18** tours. **20** top. **21** Andy. **24** WA. **25** AR.

Page 67 *1* **1** Dave Edmunds. **2** Freda Payne. **3** Paul McCartney. **4** CCS. **5** Jnr. Campbell. **6** Alice Cooper. **7** Roberta Flack. **8** Stuart Gillies. **9** George Harrison. **10** Bobby Goldsboro.

2 **1** Lee Marvin. **2** Wings. **3** Middle Of The Road. **4** Moody Blues. **5** Lynsey de Paul. **6** Guy Darrell. **7** Jethro Tull. **8** Benny Hill. **9** Michael Jackson. **10** Hot Chocolate.

3 *I Am A Clown.* **2** *Double Barrel.* **3** *Patches.* **4** *Dynamite.* **5** *Rainbow.* **6** *Sugar Sugar.* **7** *Street Life.* **8** *Step By Step.* **9** *War.* **10** *Lay Down.*

4 **1** First Choice. **2** Marmalade. **3** Middle Of The Road. **4** Rolling Stones. **5** Nazareth. **6** New York City. **7** Atomic Rooster. **8** Wings. **9** Piglets. **10** Mud.

5 **1** *Rupert.* **2** *Still Water.* **3** *January.* **4** *Girls.* **5** *Pick Up The Pieces.* **6** *Please Mr Postman.* **7** *Circles.* **8** *Paper Roses.* **9** *You're So Vain.* **10** *It Must Be Love.*

6 **1** Roxy. **2** Pilot. **3** Osmonds. **4** Slade. **5** Fox. **6** Gilstrap. **7** Labelle. **8** Gaynor. **9** Lennon. **10** Shelley.

7 **1** 1971. **2** 1973. **3** 1972. **4** 1964. **5** 1968. **6** 1975. **7** 1971. **8** 1973. **9** 1970. **10** 1973.

8 **1** a. **2** c. **3** b. **4** c. **5** a. **6** b. **7** c. **8** b. **9** b. **10** a.

9 **1** *Summer.* **2** *Alley Bred.* **3** *Save.* **4** *I Said Hello.* **5** *Of The Gang.* **6** *Softly With His Song.* **7** *Band.* **8** *Shame Shame.* **9** *Happy Song.* **10** *That You Keep.*

10 **1** Gary. **2** Peter. **3** Cat or Ray. **4** Jackie. **5** Bill. **6** Jeff. **7** Johnny. **8** Tony. **9** Desmond. **10** Helen.

11 **1** Rod Stewart. **2** Cat Stevens. **3** Clifford T. Ward. **4** Ralph McTell. **5** Mike Oldfield. **6** Status Quo. **7** Melanie. **8** Elvis Presley. **9** Donovan. **10** Neil Sedaka.

12 **1** *Candida*—all the others are tunes without words. **2** *I Say A Little Prayer*—all the other hits were recorded by men. **3** *I Love You Love Me Love*—all the other hits were recorded in 1975. **4** *Smarty Pants*—all the other hits were written by ex-Beatles.